D1630333

The Rough Side of the Boards

by the same author

Stories

Pennine Tales
Flying Eggs and Things

Non-fiction

That the Medals and Baton Be Put on View

Plays

Eh?
Stop It Whoever You Are
Big Soft Nellie
Nil Carborundum
Kelly's Eye
Good Grief!
The Little Mrs Foster Show
Honour and Offer
This Jockey Drives Late Nights
The ffinest ffamily in the Land
Pongo Plays 1–6
Six More Pongo Plays
Cinderella, a likely tale

HENRY LIVINGS

The Rough Side of the Boards

A rueful and mendacious theatrical memoir

Methuen

First published in Great Britain 1994
by Methuen London
an imprint of Reed Consumer Books Ltd
Michelin House, 81 Fulham Road, London SW3 6RB
and Auckland, Melbourne, Singapore and Toronto

Copyright © 1994 by Henry Livings
The author has asserted his moral rights

A CIP catalogue record for this title
is available from the British Library
ISBN 0 413 67860 1

Typeset by ROM-Data Corporation, Falmouth, Cornwall
Printed in Great Britain by Clays Ltd, St Ives plc

This book is sold subject to the condition
that it shall not, by way of trade or otherwise,
be lent, resold, hired out, or otherwise circulated
without the publisher's prior consent in any form
of binding or cover other than that in which
it is published and without a similar condition
including this condition being imposed
on the subsequent purchaser.

Contents

Prologue

I fell in love with Lechery at the age of nineteen. She was small, with delicate fine-boned feet and hands; otherwise, she could have been drawn in circles: round, dark eyes, head an almost perfect sphere, round shoulders, breasts, bottom, and neat round legs. She was so unlike me, with my flat size ten feet, scrawny ill-coordinated body, square heavy hands, that I had to suppose, if I thought about it at all, that it was our differences that so enveloped us in this misty, lamplit townscape of student love, as if we complemented each other.

She wasn't a very good Lechery, but she did get an Honours degree, and later a Ph.D. We were in *Dr Faustus*, presented by the Drama Society of the Liverpool Students' Guild, in which I was the scholar of the title, who sells his soul to Mephistopheles for what turns out to be a fairly poor swap: a chance to play schoolboy japes on the Pope, a chat to Helen of Troy, and a bucket-shop trip round the Seven Deadly Sins. The rest of the Sins weren't so clever either, but Marlowe gives Lechery the best lines, '. . I'd rather an inch of raw mutton than an ell of fried stockfish . .'

Faustus's final parting with his student friend was fulcral and prophetic. Mephistopheles is due to collect, and the two figures in black academic gowns and Erasmus hats shake hands for the last time . . . 'Whatsoever noise you hear, come not unto me, for nought can save me,' I said. My friend Dennis's eyes moistened, his strong pale jaw trembled briefly with manly emotion.

It was in this moment, time-locked, that I came to see that a B.A. was just two letters to nowhere, this moment contained my unfocused past and a wide, beckoning future. And anyway, Lechery had graduated and was leaving. The words of Faustus's great aria of eternal death and damnation were already running through my mind . . .

> See, see where Christ's blood streams in the firmament.
> One drop would save my soul, half a drop . . .

Dennis's lips barely moved, 'Tarah wack,' he said.

I

I begin life in the professional theatre at the top, with dustbin

I pushed at the Stage Door of the Theatre Royal, Leicester. It was divided into two . . . perhaps so as to be able to admit only one person at a time. Five foot seven, and myopic, it took me a few minutes of waiting to discover that there was a mucky white-enamelled button, marked 'bell', high up on the mucky doorframe. I pressed it. No sound came from within. A bell not to be rung, more put there as a mockery to the hopeful caller, a bell for the unremembered. I knocked.

Nine-thirty, on a Tuesday morning: you'd think *somebody*'d be about. Market stalls were being set up in the narrow lane, canvas canopies unfurled and secured. A quiet woman was laying out bric-à-brac, odd plates, impossibly large tureens, on a trestle table. A very loud man sang vigorously as he hung second-hand suits and dresses on a rail, 'O sole mio'. May, 1952. For twenty years I'd waited for this moment, ever since my first public performance. A speech composed by myself, and carefully rehearsed: 'Ladies and gentlemen, we will have jam for tea'. I'd been briefly a celebrity with family and neighbours in that drab suburban semi, and I'd liked that.

Still nobody came to the door.

I'd missed most of Coco's Crazy Car Act at Belle Vue Circus. The first entrance . . five clowns aboard a tiny brightly painted car with eccentric wheels came kangarooing and backfiring into the ring . . was so ecstatically, joyously anarchic, that seven-year-old me was soon writhing with helpless gasping weeping mirth on the floor, and had to be hauled up by my father from two rows down. And there was Coco, raising his soft brown bowler in triumph, revealing a fringe of gingery tufts and a shiny sugar-pink dome, out of which sprang a graceful jet of water. Improbable, ribald, it looked like my uncle Joe's dick in the morning; and I was off again, slithering to the floor, possessed, whirled away on a foaming torrent of glee.

I knocked again, put my ear to the door, but all I could hear was the bellowing stallholder's 'O sole mio'. I wondered if there were any more words to it. And then, there arose, among the swish of brooms and swilling water sounding out from the high windows of the Wholesale Meat and Fish Market next door to the theatre, the soaring voices of the traders as they scrubbed down after work. A woman's muscular soprano carried the verse, above a dense, largely male, hummed harmony, grand and awesome as a cathedral organ . . .

> 'The sun had set below the hill
> Across yon dreary moor
> When weary and lame, the poor man came
> Up to the farmhouse door.
> Can you, says he
> Give me employ . . .'

and now the chorus . . .

> 'For to plough and to sow
> To reap and to mow . . .'

billowing, ardently disciplined,

> 'And to be a farmer's boy-oy-oy-oy-oy
> And to be a fa-armer's BOY' (sostenuto, diminuendo).

Then the clanking of buckets, and the hiss of hoses. I rantanned on the Stage Door with vigour, tugged at it. The right-hand side was open.

I entered.

A shadowed world, one light-bulb dangled on ancient frayed flex. 'Hello?'

A very small office, just inside, just room for one bentwood chair; a black enamelled metal plate, with lettered slots for mail, one greying envelope in XYZ.

'Hello?'

Immediately beyond the office a narrow corridor stretched both ways the width of the building, the concrete floor wet from recent mopping. I didn't like to tread on a newly-mopped floor, it seemed somehow impolite; besides the man with the mop and bucket was working steadily away from me down the corridor; also I wasn't sure how my shoes, new-bought for my new job in Theatre, would stand up to the fierce, throat-clutching Jeyes Fluid. What grotesque rites and improprieties had to be so savagely cleansed?

'I keep that door shut while I mop,' said the man.

'It wasn't shut,' I said.

'I use plenty of piggin' Jeyes Fluid,' said the man, 'then they can't argue I haven't done it.'

'I was looking for Mr Dore.'

'Be on stage ten o'clock,' said the man, and mopped on.

Doors opened off the corridor, two on one side into small dressing-rooms, the plasticine smell of grease-paint; and two the other side onto a wonderland beneath the stage: broken-down furniture with sagging upholstery, costume skips, a tailor's dummy coated in dust, a cut-out plywood bush with oranges painted on it, rows of flowers with wooden brackets to prop them up, a well-head . . .

I tried to be offhand, worldly, 'I'm new,' I said, 'ASM and small parts.'

'I know full well you're new, or you wouldn't be gawping about as if you were in Buckingham Palace. My name's Ted, Ted Blunt, blunt by name and blunt by nature, and I don't give a bugger what size your parts are.'

He had the mottled eyes and unfocused authority of a veteran drill sergeant. Brown overall coat, a complexion that rarely saw daylight, the features sliding down a little from age and poor diet.

'The stage is up these stairs, Green Room's just to your left there, you can't miss it, it reeks of stale cigarette smoke.'

'Thank you.'

'Just to your right, you'll find another lot of stairs to the dressing-rooms and the fly gallery, you're not listening to what I'm saying.'

I was already half-way up to the stage.

'Go up them stairs, it's four flights, and right at the top you'll find a dustbin, under the roof. You can't miss it, it's brand piggin' new. First thing this company's ever bought new.'

That stopped me.

'It'll be full from last night's rain. There's a kazi just down from there, you can empty it into that.'

'Are you the Stage Manager?'

'I'm every piggin' thing round here.'

I set off up. I was in show business.

I'd got the job by persuading the Director to see me in a Little Theatre production (amateur). *The Lady's Not For Burning*, a costume piece, doublet and hose, and long pointy shoes. The designer had constructed a very fine medieval arch, cladding the wooden armature with chicken wire and plaster to give it an ancient, crusty look. The man playing the lead owned Elton's Fine China and Silverware, and was every bit as well-equipped for tights as Nureyev. A lady member of the group had sent a message after the dress rehearsal to say she didn't know what Ronnie had in his tights, but it was the wrong shape.

At one point in the play, I was dragged up the three steps to the arch, to be punched crisply on the jaw by the china-shop owner. The loser in most stage fights does the work; first, I had to make myself conveniently available for the swift grab to the collar; next, I had to help Ronnie drag me up for the punch by tippy-toeing up the steps; and finally, as Ronnie's fist whizzed past my jaw, I was to smack one fist into the palm of my hand, to represent the crack of knuckle on jawbone. My assailant, a compassionate man, worried that the backwards tumble down the steps was potentially dangerous, made me promise that I would open my eyes privily and give a wink, to reassure him that he hadn't accidentally demolished me.

The night the professional director dropped in, I was doubly keen that this particular moment should go well. I'd trained myself in falling, from a judo book. You distribute the impact of the fall over the whole body, simultaneously beating down with the forearms, palms down. It makes an impressive thump, and you don't break anything. Ronnie gripped me, I shot up the steps slightly irregularly because the pointy toes tangled under eager feet, so that I rose in the air before Ronnie's astonished eyes, and as swiftly down again past the flashing fist. The smack of knuckle on jawbone was a bit muffled: in the flurry, far too fast, far too close, my fist and palm had collected some of Ronnie's codpiece between. I opened my eyes as promised, and gave my confident wink.

The leading man was slumped against the medieval arch, which lurched sideways, plaster distinctly rattling down inside the armature; from backstage came the mangled anguished yelp of the scene designer, while Ronnie's eyes slowly crossed and uncrossed on a grey spinning world. The audience offered a spontaneous and respectful patter of applause, impressed by the heartfelt realism of the incident. Of such moments great drama is born; when backstage, onstage, and auditorium fuse, and all that can be known about the moment is known to all: I had buggered up a bit of business.

My future with the amateur group wasn't secure after that, Ronnie was on the Casting Committee. But the professional director thought I had promise; he told me that anyone who could levitate up three steps, take a crack on the jaw, crash down again to a stone-flagged floor with a loud hollow boom, and leave his attacker swaying and swivel-eyed, had to be a survivor. The pay would be four pounds ten shillings a week, and the contract stipulated that the artiste had to have casual clothes, a three-piece suit, dinner jacket or tails. I never saw a contract, but such was my faith that I knew for certain that that would be what the contract said, if I ever got one.

I reached the dustbin.

By it, a small bucket for baling out; above, sodden lath and plaster round a gaping hole; from the market, eighty feet below, 'O sole mio' had given way to the stentorian cliff-hanging patter of the Pot King, who would hold an immense roast-dish high with one hand, a large hammer in the other, and threaten to smash it before your eyes if it wasn't bought at one of the descending descant of prices he bellowed, 'Five-pound-and-cheap-at-the-price-four-pound-ten-you-don't-know-what-you're-missing-three-pound-nobody? threepoundthreepound . .' and crash went the hammer. That man could spiel an audience at the South Pole. 'Where you like dear,' intoned the quiet lady over her bric-à-brac, 'where you like.' Every one a public star.

I started to bucket the rainwater out of the dustbin, carrying it down to the little lavatory one narrow flight of stairs below. Much of it splattered out onto my trousers and shoes, and anyway, ten o'clock approached; so in the end I dollied the bin down from tread to tread in one go, drenching my jacket this time, and put it back empty under the leak. It intrigued me that, as I began to meet the company, nobody remarked on my sodden condition, but I soon realized they had more to think about. They played twice-nightly, with a change of play every week. There was a pecking-order; each knew, more or less, what size role would have to be learnt between the Tuesday read-through and the Friday rehearsal-without-books . . . Thursday off to learn it. There was the leading character man and lady, leading man and lady, two juveniles and two all-purpose character actors. The arrangement seemed to accommodate most scripts . . actors rarely got a week out, and it was even rarer to import extra people.

This also seemed to suit the audiences, many of whom would come week after week, on the same night, even in the same seats, and favourites would be applauded vigorously on first sight. Backstage, I learned how this was done. Frank, the leading man, always well-dressed and groomed, short, slightly bandy, and with one eye that wandered very slightly, so that his comedy timing was subtly enhanced . . as if Ben Turpin should play the Chaplin part. When the cue for his first entrance came, he would set off briskly for the door, then take two steps back, and set off again; a small, neat ritual offstage dance which meant that everyone on stage was turned to watch the door, and concentrated mightily on Frank for two or three vibrant seconds; the psychic power of his absence communicated to all like an unspoken, tingling mantra: 'Where's Frank?'; then he was on, warm applause; everybody was glad to see Frank on stage, including Frank.

There was no read-through as such, no discussion of the play's meaning or the characters, as I had experienced at university; more of a walk-through . . . nobody had read more than was needed to underline their own role. In pencil. The scripts had to go back to French's afterwards . . another job I acquired, rubbing out the pencil marks. During which chore I noticed that in farces, there were sometimes asterisks which, a note indicated, was 'Show-stopping laugh, if played correctly'. I resolved to watch the company very very closely, especially Frank. The plays were mostly ex-West End fodder, light comedies, thrillers, farce, taken on trust because they'd done well in the West End; and in any case, the actors knew their work much in the way any artisan learns his in his apprentice days: there's one unfailing way to deal with any given task; they might have to be reminded, but they knew it. Like: Big speech equals be upstage for it, preferably standing. 'Scissors', with two actors crossing the stage at the same time and in opposite directions, equals bad news, the audience won't know which way to focus their attention. Exit line: make sure your hand is on the doorknob. 'It's been nothing but cabbage cabbage cabbage ever since I came to this house, and anyway (wait for it) your sink stinks.' (Exit, slam door, and be sure it *stays* shut.)

The cast walked about, script and pencil in hand, jotting down the moves as the Director proposed them, or as they themselves found to be right; 'x to w.p.b.', i.e. 'Cross to waste paper basket' (and Reg, the Stage Manager, added w.p.b. to his props list). Some of this 'blocking', I found, was to pre-empt the steady upstaging of fellow-actors. But the older hands had a countergambit to this. As the Ego edged upstage, they would find it necessary to gaze thoughtfully out front as they delivered their lines, leaving the perpetrator isolated, with only backs to talk to, like a man at a party with a *very* funny story no one wants to hear. More importantly the memorized moves gave them marker-buoys, something to cling on to in the tide-race of story and dialogue barely remembered or understood. They were survivors.

However, in this, my very first show, there was a hiccup. An actress had been booked to join the company to rehearse for the following week, and it had been comfortably assumed that she'd play a walk-on maid that evening. We were trudging through a lighting and technical rehearsal, and she hadn't shown. Informed opinion was that she must have stepped off the London train, and seen the poster telling her she was to be playing twice-nightly; she would then have walked right back through the barrier to catch the next train back to the Smoke. By Equity agreement, the pay for working twice as hard was a third again on the Agreed Minimum Terms.

Meanwhile Pam, as the Duchess in her stately home, was going to have to hurtle off and get her own tea-tray, and she wasn't pleased. Neither was Frank, who would be standing there like a lemon while she did it. The Front of House Manager was set to phoning round his occasional staff for a mug. They all had to be mugs to work for the money he paid, but one of the usherettes was stage-struck, and she was easily persuaded to take an afternoon off work to rehearse. She had to carry on a large silver tea-tray set with elegant china, put it down, and exit. I was appointed to give the nudge when her cue came, and make sure she went on by the right door. I reflected, when I had the time, that I might not be getting much stage experience, but I was certainly piling up the jobs.

The young lady had also been an usherette at the Empire, the touring theatre, and had an extensive acquaintance with the stars, with many an anecdote. 'Jack', I worked out, was probably John Gielgud; 'Larry' and 'Viv' were easy enough, but 'Rafe' had me baffled. It was clear she had an altogether different notion of theatre to my own. She looked on it as more like royalty-watching; she touched the hem of glory and was the grander person for it. She'd rattled on to an account of her success as Oedipus's mother in the School Play . . . 'Who's Rafe?' I asked. She paused, glanced, said, 'Your trousers is sodden,' and relaunched herself at the point where Miss Rackstraw was moved to tears by Oedipus's plight in Wigston.

I was prompter, a fairly easy job for my first professional show; the book was clearly marked by Reg, with Stand-bys for such as act curtains and lighting cues. First house, Act Two . . . we always had three acts, for the bar sales. In the welter of new events, I didn't notice that the tyro actress had taken hold of the tray by the side-handles, instead of presenting it to the doorway the narrow way, as rehearsed. She'd ad-libbed a curtsey that afternoon, so she wasn't without resource. I tapped her on the shoulder as her cue came up, and hurried back round to the Prompt Corner. I became aware that a strange new atmosphere had been born in my brief absence. Frank and Pam continued with their aristocratic exchanges, the Home Counties at bay with their own battened-down emotions, but it had become halting, more like a surrealist happening, where reality lies elsewhere, the phrases isolated from each other; the Duke and Duchess struggled with a glazed bewilderment.

Upstage of them, in the doorway, a scuffling reality had overtaken polished artifice. The maid, and the audience with her, debated her problem: thirty-inch doorhole, thirty-inch tray, plus knuckles. From the audience, small squeals of happiness escaped suppression. Frank and Pam finally had no choice but to give the young star her golden moment. She tried tilting the tray gingerly. Milk slopped from the silver jug (courtesy of Elton's, Fine China and Silver), lumps of sugar toppled gently. Tried tilting it the other way; the tea-set slid smartly down the lubricating milk, and halted like guardsmen, just in time. She turned and backed in, her charming black-draped rump, with a bow of frothy white apron strings, bucking and swaying as the tray refused the door again. I could hear tip-up seats clunk amid shouts and squeaks of Dionysiac joy as the audience helped each other back onto their seats. The circus was back in town.

Suddenly, Reg, the Stage Director was there, his face and hair glowing flame-red in the backstage doorstrip light; he snatched the tray from her hands, thrust it back at her, correctly aligned, propelled her on, reached in for the door, and slammed it shut behind her. Through sweat-streaked wisps of hair, the maid looked around, an expression of mulish panic in her eyes that went clear to the upper circle. She advanced to the coffee table on stilted legs, laid down the tumble of crocks, awash with tea and milk and a grey mud of sugar, strode back upstage centre, remembered the curtsey, ducked under the arch of the vast fireplace, and disappeared from public view. Cheerful applause. Frank's double-takes continued for minutes after her kamikaze exit, and came near to winning a standing-ovation.

First absolute of theatre: doing it successfully is not at all the same thing as doing it well. As far as the audience was concerned, she was still up the chimney at the play's end. Reg took over in the corner to signal the curtain calls to Ted: 'Find that silly mare and get her on for the Who's Best,' he said.

She was sitting in the small onstage dressing-room among brooms.

'Come on,' I said, 'they thought you were marvellous, a good laugh.'

Tears gouted from her eyes, and she shook her head vigorously, 'No I bloody shan't,' she shouted.

'It's unprofessional to miss the curtain-call, a sackable offence, I bet,' I said, unsure.

'You've got some room to talk, at least I don't wet my pants!'

So that was how I got my first professional acting part, and learned many a lesson, including one tip from Frank. 'If you're planning a double-take,' he told me, 'make sure you're looking in the other direction.' The audiences, many of whom had been told by friends to look out for the comic maid in Act Two, were a little puzzled by my stand-in manservant, but there were small laughs to be had still, and they seemed contented enough. Pam was less charitable. 'What's this laugh we're getting when you bring on the tea-tray,' she said, 'it's a serious scene, and you keep glancing up from that tray, and they laugh.'

'Well,' I said, 'you're still calling me "Elsie". I look up from the tray, and then back again.'

'It's that bloody Frank,' she said, 'I'll kill him.'

2

Actor v. Collar; Scene Designer v. Frighteningly Helpful Little Old Lady

Frank lay in a splayed bundle on the floor of his dressing-room hanging cupboard, his feet straight out before him. His glittering shoes, and the sharp creases of his trousers reminded me that here lay the dapper leading man, but the rest of him was wrecked like the last hour of a New-to-You sale. His shoulders were hunched among suits, his eyes bulged, one side of his detached collar stood up against his cheek, the glowing black waves of his hair stuck out round his head in limp Brylcreem fronds. Then he drew up a leg in an attempt to rise. Ten-thirty, Saturday night.

The scene had stopped me as I hurried along the corridor under the stage. I went in and hoisted Frank upright. He indicated wordlessly that he needed to sit down, so I helped him to the ancient *chaise longue*, where the actor stretched himself, gasping painfully.

'Pam?' I said.

Frank shook his head, 'Collar,' he croaked.

Most of the actors wore paper collars for the show, but I could see that the one Frank was wearing now was an expensive Trubenized one, presumably ready for the dash to catch the late London train. A paper one lay torn in the waste bin. Stage makeup was heavy, to compensate for the crude, blaring footlights, spots and floods, which reversed the shadows, distorting the features like Dracula. Photos of Max Miller give an idea of the fluorescent appearance of the old artistes, but you could nevertheless tell they were human beings; the imagination of the audience adjusted instantly to the heightened realism, as readily as at seven years old I had accepted Coco's painted smile. Paper collars could be thrown away when they got dirty, whereas cotton ones would be indelibly stained, ingrained with Leichner flesh tones, greased beyond the reach of soap.

The dressing-room was silent, except for Frank's intermittent gargle. Above us, the scrape and thump of the Saturday night strike, which is where I was supposed to be, but I was thinking it might be useful to my understanding of drama if I discovered the hidden hazards lurking in a paper collar. Frank was groping at the collar. I tried to help him undo it, but Frank waved me away stoically. The top seemed to be missing from the stud, another mystery.

'Shall I call a doctor?'

Again the brave gesture that others had a greater need. 'Get back to the strike, or else nobody'll ever get to bed ever again.'

By the time I reached the stage, this week's set had been struck and stacked, and next week's was beginning to take shape. A stripped stage, under a couple of bare-bulb working lights, and a dark empty auditorium smelling of dust and departed people. At such times, it's easy to imagine a theatre is haunted. I turned to bring on next week's furniture. Behind me, a quiet, sepulchral whimper. I spun again. In the shadows, Gwyn, the designer, usually calm and sunny under stress, was gibbering. There seemed to be a lot of anguish about tonight, and not much explanation for it.

To put up a stage set with any dispatch, it really needs three people. One fore and one aft to lift the flat off the stack and run it up to its mark; then the one at the front snakes the cord up in a loop, so that it curls round and grips the top two cleats, draws it tight, bringing the edges of the two flats together and tying off round the bottom two cleats. Meanwhile, the third stage-hand is helping to bring the next flat from the stack. There's a rhythm to it, and the set seems to grow organically before your eyes.

Gwyn only had two complete sets of scenery, one was onstage for the current show, the other being painted for next week. After years of use, and no time at all to scrub off the accumulated layers of scene-paint, the surface of the canvas had developed the flaky texture of a dried cow-pat. You had to be careful how you closed a door during a show: if you were too heavy-handed, pictures on the walls near by would flap and settle, jostling scales of dry paint off, giving a Hogarthian aspect to the scene.

So Gwyn was happiest when the set went up fast, while the paint still held a little moisture and would stand up to the handling. In my absence, Gwyn had had to help the other two; now he was free to step back and make sure all the flats were in the correct order, and doors and windows where they'd been rehearsed. One flat out of the three now up had its shadows painted the wrong way round. Gwyn was chewing his knuckles.

It certainly looked odd, like one of those newspaper

photographs of the moon's surface where you struggle to work out what's mountain and what's crater. Gwyn wasn't without imagination, on the contrary, he could conjure miracles on canvas, had to. But here his artifice was revealed for what it was, phoney, and what's worse, a failed and incomprehensible phoney. 'Fiddle-de-fuck,' he murmured.

Gwyn's love of theatre and things theatrical saw him through many a trial. And he'd been sorely tested the previous weekend. He'd visited a group of friends in his previous company in Stockport, and they'd seen him off at the station. Friends, like family, are never so jolly as when they're saying goodbye, and they'd come up with a merry prank, which might well have the additional benefit of getting him a table to himself, and a peaceful undisturbed journey. They chaired him along the platform, with that loud, grating good humour that people often use towards the afflicted. They bought him jelly babies and comics, 'Did you get those with the big coloured pictures? I dare say someone will read them out to you, but you like the pictures don't you Gwynnie? There, you can tell he's pleased.' Gwyn's suppressed giggles and snorts did indeed seem like the infantile happy gurgles of the retarded.

As the porters were slamming doors closed along the train, and his friends were popping a last sweetie into Gwyn's helpless mouth . . 'Find him a green one, You Like The Green Ones Best Don't You Gwynnie-winnie?' . . reassuring any other passenger bold enough to come near that he would be met at Leicester, they mustn't worry; they'd made sure he'd done his number ones and his number twos before he left the Home, but if he wanted to go on the train, he could usually manage on his own . . a charming and slightly out of breath old lady, with many a bag and parcel, eased herself apologetically past the friends, and into the seat opposite Gwyn.

Time went into overdrive before Gwyn's frightened eyes, as the farewell party backed hastily for the door, Judases all, the whistle blew, and they hurled themselves from the departing train, with small uncertain waves to Gwynnie-winnie as the train glided past them on the platform. How much had the old lady heard? how much had she seen of the charade? The sweeties and the comic books on the seat by him weren't all that visible, and anyway, they could be presents for some child at his destination.

He groped a hand out furtively at the evidence of his disabilities, a sweetie bag fell to the floor, he closed his eyes in silent prayer. When he opened them, the lady was smiling a small, kind smile at him. 'I'm going to Leicester too,' she said, 'we can be company for each other.' She reached down painfully for the sweetie bag, and retrieved it, put it on the table between them. 'The green ones you like isn't it?' She found a green jelly baby and pushed it into his mouth, now set in a rictus of terror. She knew.

In these long, long, racing milliseconds, there must have been a moment at which he could have sloughed-off the appalling persona his friends had bequeathed him. The formula of words for such an admission escaped him like fallen leaves in an eddy of wind.

'It was their little joke,'

Whose little joke? He was in the middle, wasn't he? He was a grown man, grown men don't play silly buggers in public, unless it's a pub trip, and everybody knows what's going on. Suppose she was even now comparing his development with that of a grandchild who was yet to speak clearly at four years old?

All his young life he'd been trained to respect old ladies, not to contradict, be *nice*. Old ladies were Devon cream and warm scones, crocheting as they sat among birdsong in fragrant summer gardens on long, warm, still afternoons. 'Such a *nice* boy.' As he wrestled with his tormenting dilemma, she was taking out a small and well-thumbed book, and settled to read to him, in quiet, well-modulated tones. Clearly she knew how to communicate with the unformed mind. A backward daughter? Oh God.

'My daughter loved this one, when she was a child, she was always very grown-up, and now she has a daughter of her own, and I'm taking her this. It's *The Tale of Two Bad Mice*,' she said, and read relentlessly on, as Gwyn planned his escape at Derby, where he knew they had to change trains.

The Ticket Inspector was a grim and terrible experience. He waited with genial nodding patience, winking at Gwyn as the old lady rooted through his jacket pockets for his ticket, found it for him and handed it over to be punched. She also came across his booklet of homoerotic photographs, an irreplaceable collector's item, and trotted off to find a waste bin, tearing it up as she went.

'The human body is a thing of beauty,' she remarked to the inspector, 'but it's hardly to be dwelt on.'

She found the right platform for the Leicester train. He had a vague recollection that the gents on Derby station had exits on both sides, and this was going to be his escape route: in one door, out the other, and wait for the next train for Leicester. He gripped his holdall, and indicated mutely where he was going. She enquired if he was quite sure he could manage on his own, but he was on his way. 'Don't be too long, Gwynnie-winnie,' she called after him, 'our train will be here in *five minutes*. Now we know what five minutes means don't we?'

Her matronly concern faded mercifully as he turned the tiled wall inside that masked the view and the sounds from the platform. There was only one exit, the one by which he had just entered, and outside of which stood the old lady. Would she catch the train, and release him from this nightmare? The gents was ill-lit; the floor gleamed wet under a single barred lamp; a message on the wall above the urinal said 'Nobby Stiles has Piles, and Matt Busby is Shit.' It was a place of dank despair.

'All right are we old chap?'

An elegantly pinstriped man, with briefcase. A smell of Old Spice as he approached Gwyn, bejeaned, slim, and dreadfully alone. The man edged cautiously closer, reached out a hand, and patted Gwyn's shoulder to direct him towards the stones. 'In a bit of trouble are we?' Gwyn groaned his assent, reached out a hand, blind with anxiety, to touch the man's cheek, a slight stubble, and now Pear's Soap. 'Affectionate beggars, often,' murmured the man, as he guided Gwyn, whose legs were shaky and unsteady under him, 'easy does it, old chap.' The man's hands were brisk at Gwyn's flies. No trouble to find his prick, it flirted out like a quivering ashplant. Oh the comfort of that clean, friendly hand. 'Shame, shame,' muttered the man, sentimental. 'Grown healthy body, with a child's mind in charge.'

Gwyn's mind, and what's more his senses were

swimming, the man's words hardly impinged, though he remembered them later with a scalding clarity. What a place to score, between trains in Derby station cottage; he rested his grateful head on the man's broad shoulder, trembling . . . Please God don't let the kindly old lady send someone in to help him pee . . . He reached out a hand, faint, for the businessman's trousers . . . 'Everything all right?' The kindly old lady, discreet but urgent, close by the concealing wall at the door to the platform. 'I don't think he wants to go ma'am,' called the man, struggling to get Gwyn's dong back into his Y-fronts . . 'The train's coming now Gwynnie-winnie,' she called . .

He was delivered back to his tormentor, zipped-up, his bum crooked back curiously to keep his painfully erect tip from contact with the zip.

It's probable that many a cheerful, even-tempered exterior covers a menagerie of apprehensions, and certainly for months after his plunge into Edgar Allan Poe Gwyn had wondered if his early imprint of dainty matrons didn't mask his fears of the world's brutalities and his own vulnerability: their warm and ample bosoms carried vipers. If one such approached, benign, in a crowded street, he would suddenly find a windowful of surgical appliances of riveting interest until they'd passed.

Porters, for instance, are not easily found on Leicester station; she found two, to stuff his pockets with comics and sweeties, and to guide his stumbling feet up the stairs to the Booking Hall, and out to find the friends she knew were to meet him. Ignoring the queue at the taxi rank, Gwyn leapt, galvanic from their grip, and into the back of the first cab before it had stopped, with a wild yelp of 'Theatre Royal!'

He heard her fading 'Goodbye, Gwynnie-winnie', as the car moved smoothly off, and glanced round in time to see her spreadeagled in a dead faint among her parcels on the pavement.

Reg decided I could make us all a cup of tea while Gwyn made up his mind what to do about the flat which didn't sort with the surrounding, carefully-painted illusion of solid wall. 'And where were you when we needed you?' Reg said. 'I found Frank collapsed in his dressing room.' Led by Reg, Ted and I trooped downstairs, careful not to spill our mugs of tea. Frank had cleaned off his makeup by now, leaving him the colour of lead pipe, still no collar. Frank without a collar looked nude. 'Where's the collar?' said Reg. 'I'm giving them up, for life,' said Frank, 'I've missed the London train.' He looked and sounded to be in terminal despair. I couldn't quite see that missing the London train was all that much of a disaster, nor can I now.

'It's got to be Pam that did this,' said Ted. 'She's the only one that can stand up to you pansies. She knows who put the Stilton round the dado. So she'd have to move out of the upstairs front while the landlady got the Health in. Well you've got it, and see where it's got you. She liked that room, it was near the lav.' 'God she's common,' whispered Frank to no one in particular. 'She's everlasting pittling, that's all,' said Ted. 'Went to a convent school, and the nuns wouldn't let her leave the room, so now she's everlasting having to leave the room.

Fine body of a woman, mind.' He picked his nose thoughtfully, oblivious of Frank's distress. Eleven-thirty by now, his overtime was looking good.

Gwyn called down from the top of the stairs, 'I've repainted the three-foot,' he said, 'and it's up. And balls to the lot of you.'

Frank spoke as if from behind drifting mist, 'In order to catch the eleven-four, I play the last scene as far as possible in garments that will be acceptable on public transport. I leave the makeup off under my chin, so as not to smear my revers inadvertently . . .' His every move and every word were carefully calculated, I had already discovered, both on and off stage. In an uncertain world, Frank created his own small certainty. 'I then shoot down here,' he continued, 'after the Who's Best, rip away the paper collar, clean off the remaining makeup, put on a sturdy and elegant Trubenized, and depart at speed for the train. Tonight's show over-ran.'

'Yes?' said Reg, who knew full well, having written it down in the Report Book himself.

'Ripped off the collar, thinking it was still the paper one. It wasn't.'

Frank's wandering eye seemed to go off on an extra little wander, in search, perhaps, of some way of impressing the others with the seriousness of his suffering. 'I thought I'd ruptured my oesophagus; the front stud held it just long enough to double the impact, gave way, and there I was, flat on my back.'

'I'll get you another collar-stud, out of wardrobe,' I said.

'Please die now,' said Frank, 'before my eyes. It'd be a comfort.'

3

Youth is wasted on the young, but how was I to know that?

Lechery was to sail to New York. I never understood the fierce family pressure exerted on her. She told me her parents stormed against the relationship, yet still I wrote. I'd take a hopeful pile of pennies to the Stage Door phone. 'She's not answering the phone', 'You must have a wrong number', and eventually just a click as the receiver was replaced. Yet still I phoned, and still came away with the same pile of pennies. Less tuppence. What an egregious ass. If ever I had a glimmer that to most people, a degree is a passport to security, prosperity, respectability, I certainly don't remember it, and never came to any understanding that security, prosperity, respectability were worth having in the first place.

Then she found a job in London, with a rare-books dealer. Two concentration camp survivors had clawed their way from refugee camp, with nothing but hand-me-down suits they were given, and the blue tattooed numbers on their forearms, to buy the business in Regent Street. Much of their success came from breaking up early printed books, called incunabula, and framing individual pages so that both sides could be seen. This sounds like vandalism, but it seems that the big collectors aren't much interested in incomplete incunabula, whereas wealthy and aspirant young bourgeois, keen to add some scholarly and elegant antiquity to the damask Regency stripes and reproduction Chippendale of their mews flats, would pay good guineas for a unique scintilla of exquisitely illuminated history, even if they didn't know what it said.

The partners had found a mutton-headed scion of the minor aristocracy, and offered him a partnership. He dressed well (which they didn't), but no doubt his tailor and his valet attended to that, and he was also very good at taxis. Otherwise his sole and indispensable contribution to the business lay in exclaiming, in the presence of a well-heeled mark, 'My word, what an extremely interesting example, fourteenth-century is it? I think so, Flemish, I should say.' The partners also had an outlet in New York. The blue tattooed numbers were a sign that these were men who would not go back, and neither would she.

I took an early Sunday train, straight from the overnight set-up at the theatre. A couple of hours' sleep in the Green Room, but I was still grey and shaky. I was lucky in that my father wore good lightweight suits for work, and they got spoilt eventually by the rubber solvent: tiny holes, not visible from the auditorium, but which made them unsuitable for middle management. For me, that meant I could comfortably and for free meet the requirements of the contract, if I ever got one: formal suit and casual to be provided by the artiste. The dinner suit would be a problem, but I'd saved steadily during my stint as *pâtissier* at the Bell Hotel. Twelve pounds the tuxedo, and now my weekly wage was four pounds ten shillings. And still I didn't see the insanity of the life I'd chosen.

So, there I was, platform two, Leicester railway station, hoping the daylight wouldn't shine like stars through my diaphanous tweeds. The train was late, passengers for later ones were beginning to filter onto the platform, shuffling, uneasy and strained, stepping out every so often to gaze up the empty line. I had time to reflect on her letters, which told of her new oddball life, the way time's cratered fields could contain the jewelled inks of dead monks, and the rich composting debris of survivors. A new world, which was as rich as it was cruel and desolate.

During my basic training at RAF Wilmslow, I'd been witness to the merciless baiting by NCOs of a boy from the Scottish Isles, who had been sewn into his long-johns for the winter. And I'd watched the drill pig doubling an overweight recruit back and forth across the vast parade ground, 'Yew lardy guzzling erk! Double up double up double double double ay-bout tun! By the time I've finished with yew yew 'orrible airman yew will be a lean killing machine or else yew will be *dead*!' And at night, through the lighted billet window, I saw the drill pig jerkily and silently snarling his commands, hands clenching and unclenching in demented rhythm; I saw these deranged cruelties as temporary, for six weeks only. For the two book dealers, savage and brutal indifference was the permanent furniture of their lives. No safety-net, no sustaining comradeship, no family. Anywhere. I had an uneasy feeling that the laughter I thought so important might be a grim rattle in the throat of death.

My own parents were of the generation that began to detach itself from the family network, and seemed to expect me to detach myself from them. It was already showing in pre-war advertising, gas and electric cookers, vacuum cleaners, gadgets which would release the housewife, get her out into the world. They didn't. For one thing, there weren't a lot of jobs to get out into. But the war did. Serving relatives would visit on brief leaves, but the atmosphere was subdued. Where before there had been songs round the piano – Uncle Frank straining earnestly for the top notes of 'Juanita'; Auntie Margaret meticulously constructing a splendid family row by her pub habit of leaving her lighted cigarette on the right-hand top keys as she played – now the uniformed figures were remote, their business and their lives elsewhere, in Spartan, sealed military camps, the loneliness of shared violence and danger.

Grandma was the exception, a constant. I had quite a strong bond with her; in her company, I got a glimpse of what family life could be, full of old certainties. She worked, from getting up, a cup of tea to hand, a Woodbine kippering her moustache, to nightfall as she knitted socks by the wireless. The same tasks at the same time, each to its day, baking bread, the family wash, the entire house cleaned to the bottom, the Sunday roast . . each carried out to a maddening invisible standard. The household would wind up to a tense controlled hysteria as she knitted. I could feel the tension rising as she approached the heel. Father's cigarette consumption went steadily up, and strain screwed pulsing lines round his jaw. When I thought the house might finally explode, Grandma would spot the mistake in her knitting, and release her long-awaited wail 'Oooh Dorothy . . .' And begin unravelling the entire sock, and then wind the wool round a milk bottle, steam it straight, and start again. By this time, Father was in the garden, digging. Even if it was dark, he'd be digging.

Above all, Grandma was a constant, as certain as Big Ben. Both my parents worked long hours in Manchester, my dad making barrage balloons and tank tyres, and then a fire-watcher at night; my mother a telephonist for the Fire Brigade. If I went straight home from school, it was to a pencilled list of shopping, clean out the grate, and mind you take those mucky shoes off, the house cold, the neighbours strangers who only looked out through their net curtains if they heard the tinkle of the telegraph boy's bell: was it a telegram from France? North Africa? India? 'His Majesty regrets . . .'

If Grandma wasn't there, from as soon as I could walk, I would escape from that dank, neat, suburban garden, with its grimy gritty rockery, to distant, wild, neglected and overgrown paradise among ferns and brambles above the flat industrial reaches of the Irwell Valley, the soapworks, the power station, the shunting yards, the fever hospital, each darkening the air with their dense black smoke, poisoning the river so that to swim there was suicidally dangerous. Among those ferns and stunted trees, I was as lost, and as deeply fulfilled as I was under the seats at the circus, when Coco filled my universe with fireworks.

As I waited for the London train, I became aware of a small silver-haired man, in a tailored black overcoat, who carried a well-worn leather pouch in a grip that made his knuckles white. He was benign, neat, gave small cheerful nods about him, not to anyone particular, more general. As the platform grew more crowded, the gentlemanly old gentleman edged imperceptibly forward to the edge. It was a small scene, on the edge of my field of vision, but none the less riveting.

I thought I'd found some vestigial certainties, for a few hours of a long working day, I was somebody, a part of something. And they were slipping away, these certainties were not so sure.

Were her letters attempts to paper over deep differences between us. Or to reveal them in a clear light to both of us? Her willed rejection of her background, deliberately building another one at school and university; my drab background filled with unformulated hopes, the soot-laden privet hedges beyond which there must be a richer life. The grammar school which opened so many doors for her, and mine that threatened to lock doors, to direct me to serve and even join the Establishment, the officer class, in whose ranks my shabby teachers so fervently wished to stand. A cold hand closed round my heart at the thought that she might be wanting to tell me that our differences were too great. She might be right, and I didn't want to find out.

The train steamed slowly in at last, and I moved forward with the weary crowd. As soon as the train had stopped, the old gentleman seized a door handle, and a neat black polished shoe came down on mine with a bone-crushing impact. Other passengers streamed busily by me as I checked how much use I still had in my foot. By the time I got aboard, most seats were taken, but I found one by the corridor. Across from me in the window seat, facing the engine, the old gentleman nodded to me as to a brief acquaintance he couldn't quite place, then took out a white linen handkerchief to wipe a space clear on the slimy window. The starched cuff fell back, and a pale chicken-bone wrist was revealed briefly. There was no tattooed number. And then the hands were folded meekly again on the tailored lap.

The carriage reeked like a room that's been locked up for years, the rolling stock clanked and lurched. In my mind, I saw the steel and concrete canyons of New York, the scurrying black and white figures of the newsreels, the grinding menace of the Elevated Railway. Then a long landscape, from horizon to horizon, trudging lines of heavy ragged overcoats. I'd seen it in 1947, when I went as a volunteer to help clear war rubble in Vienna. I'd been set to shovel wagon-loads of bricks and twisted metal down a huge tip on the outskirts of the city. A woman refugee was on the same job, the nearest thing to a human cube I'd ever come across. Even when I'd been potato-picking in Lincolnshire I'd never seen such a solid physique, such a powerful frame. She shovelled like a machine, unceasing, only pausing to move to the next wagon. Then, suddenly she stopped, straightened, and pointed with a hand as broad as her shovel towards the distance, for all the world like a bronze Monument to Labour. The flat plain below us seemed to stretch for hundreds of miles, until it was finally bounded by mountains. 'Hun-ga-ree,' she said, with stolid longing.

I was becoming aware that the world was opening up, even as the theatre closed round me. Wider than the tall Texan soldiers my grandfather entertained in 1943. Our

Brave Allies, the old man puffing on their enormous Cuban cigars, pillaging the bitter chocolate from the K-rations they brought, sucking greedily at their Kentucky sourmash. The world was opening up, even the dark narrow streets of commercial Manchester, opened to wide skies by the Blitz.

I rehearsed my unanswerable riddle for the old gentleman, egregiously determined to make a stand for individual dignity and self-respect. 'In the world of the dung-beetle,' I said, clear across to the other corner, 'which is the better, the dungball or the beetle?' That should let the old bastard know. The old man seemed serenely unaware that he'd just been compared to a dung-beetle, or else to a ball of dung, and hutched forward in his seat for conversation. The other passengers thanked their luck that the loonie hadn't picked on them, and lifted Sunday newspapers for closer inspection.

'In my home town in Poland,' said the old man, 'there was a Talmudic scholar and thinker, whose wisdom and knowledge was so great that his students held him in profound reverence. However, they, as callow and foolish young men, decided to put the old man to a test. He was very poor, as many great thinkers must be, such is the way of things. He was delighted when they invited him to a fine meal. During the meal, they made sure he drank a large amount of wine, so that in the end, he fell asleep. Then, they carried him to the cemetery, where they knew there was a new-dug grave, still open, and laid the great man in it. They withdrew a little distance, and waited patiently to see what deep perception would emerge from the philosopher when he awoke in such a place. After a very long time, a tranquil voice floated up out of the grave. "If I am alive, why am I here?" said their great teacher, "and if I am dead, why do I want to go to pee?" ' The world was opening up, and I blinked in the unforgiving light of my own fatuity.

She was at the downstairs door to her Swiss Cottage bedsit before I'd raised my hand to knock. We shared a conviction that each knew when we were going to meet the other, even if it was by accident. I had to half-admit to myself that there was a possibility that she'd been watching out for me from her window, or that she knew the time of my train. I preferred the conviction. The door panels and frame were glazed with small leaded lights, the colours of cheap wine-gums, the floor of the hallway was yellow and brick-red terrazzo, a gloomy, cold place, but as I closed the door behind me, there began a brief, radiantly simple life, for twenty-four sweet-tasting hours. There were no awkward angles or rough edges to our embraces. I was no longer the victim of my own overweening enthusiasm, pushing myself forward where there was no gap and my presence was not sought. She was no longer the Best Girl in the Class, smiling the reflex smile that masks uncertainty. We didn't even entangle our glasses.

We walked on Primrose Hill in misty sunshine, and wondered if that was the dome of St Paul's we could see, and was that the shimmering Skylon, silver tethered phallus of the Festival of Britain site? We went to the Zoo, and communed with Guy, the infinitely melancholy and dignified mountain gorilla, still as carved ebony.

Perhaps drawn by our rapt attention, the keeper came to stand by our side. 'I can't go in his cage when he's there,' he said, 'not no more. I used to sit with him, for hours, helping him to calm down after the day. People are cruel, taunt him. They don't mean to be cruel, but they shout suddenly, and show off, laugh among themselves. Throw peanuts, to see if he'll move. He wouldn't harm me. It's just that he hugs me, see, and won't let me out again to go home. Grinning teeth, shouting and laughing, is a threat to Guy.'

She wore a white nightgown, made of some gossamer material, rosy from her bath. Sixpence in the gas meter, and you had to be fast before it went cold. I put my arms round her and led her to the wardrobe mirror. 'Are you sometimes proud of your beauty?' She smiled a small smile wondering if I guessed at all the careful preparation, the leg-shaving, eyebrow-plucking, the astringent and the cream. I used the bathwater after her, as I had my sister's as a child, in that freezing Manchester bathroom. Here the bathroom was like a steam oven, she must have damn near scalded herself.

'Where's the soap gone?'

'I'll get you a fresh one.'

'There was soap here before. I washed my hands with it earlier.'

'It'd got dirty cracks in it. I threw it away.'

In bed, she remarked on the miraculous fit of male and female, even as her leftover arm began to ache, and had to be withdrawn.

In the morning, I packed to leave and then we embraced clumsily, gorilla and keeper, bonded by an impossible and uncomprehending need. When she drew back, her face was crumpled and scarlet, shining wet, as if every part of her wept helplessly. 'I'll never see you again,' she said, and I couldn't bear the crooked, gawky grin I knew was distorting my mouth. I was trying to reassure her, but couldn't work out the terms, couldn't envisage happiness as a permanent condition, except for idiots. My life was full of absences, hers full of tyrannical presences. She was tearing herself loose, I'd never been attached since the cord was cut. Until now. Perhaps my twisted grin contained some smugness that I could be the cause of such overwhelming emotion. I couldn't bear that either, and went wooden into the morning, without looking back.

The silver-haired gentleman was on the platform at Euston already, the leather pouch now folded flat under his arm. I imagined a scenario of diamonds prised from unredeemed pawned engagement rings, changing hands in small dusty offices in the City, picked over and weighed in brass scales polished by long use: old dreams, from commerce to young love and back again in one lifetime. My sage reflections were once again subverted by the gentlemanly old gentleman. 'The young philosopher no less,' he said, 'are you going to give us your thought for today as we travel along? How do you like "The gods send nuts to men with no teeth"?' I wished I'd bought myself a morning paper.

As the Leicester train slowed down to a halt, I eased myself forward among the waiting travellers into a gap by the old man's side, even as he moved forward . . he seemed to know to an inch at which point there would be a door. I opened the door, stood back momentarily as if to allow others to go first, my heel firmly and hard on the shiny black toecap beside me, using it as a purchase to spring aboard, and took a window seat in the first compartment, facing the engine, looking straight before me. A paltry revenge, but no less satisfying for that.

The old man followed me after a moment, and limped to the seat opposite me, nodding polite greetings all round the carriage; he laid the pouch on the seat under the arm, swivelled awkwardly, like a graceless marionette, turning round to sit, bent briefly, straightened again, and sat down. There was a metallic click-click, distinct and quiet among the rowdy banging of doors, the bellowing of porters, and the shriek of steam-whistles outside. Then another click-click as the man drew the leg up with both hands and settled it next to the other. He seemed not to notice the crushed and scoured toecap of his shoe. As he sat back, he caught my eye on him, nodded and smiled, 'Sticks a bit in damp weather,' he said.

The lush, deep pastures of Buckinghamshire slid by, the pheasant copses, the comfortable, big-legged Friesian and Hereford cows undisturbed by the train's violent passage, rabbits on the embankments raised nosey noses and hopped idly on. For me, the scene had the relentless, featureless vastness of the steppes. I was alone, and the landscape was too big, not people-sized. For an Englishman, in a country which ends abruptly and soon whichever way you walk, the horizons are oceanic; the clanking steam-engines powered coasters, transatlantic liners (she was going, she was leaving) and cargo boats. I could hear the greedy screaming laments of seagulls that we'd listened to together by the Mersey, the deep unmodulated blare of the fog-horn at Pierhead, as if Guy had a voice sufficient to his wrongs. And I couldn't bear that either.

She threw away the soap because it was dirty.

4

The astounding effects of stage effects, and a clash of theatre fashion

As it happened, the clanging that most brought my loss to mind was made by the gigantic roller I'd arranged to borrow from the Leicester Parks and Gardens Department. I'd emptied the rainwater from the dustbin at the top of the stairs, and my next job was to collect the roller, which was to trundle across wooden slats nailed to the stage floor for the train effect in *Ghost Train*. Any metaphor would have done to echo the majesty of that departing liner, there wasn't much else on my mind, but the roller, with the massive inevitability of its momentum, was poignant and unstoppable enough for me.

The Parks Manager was doubtful. He looked at my scrawny frame and said the roller had never been outside the De Montfort Gardens since its delivery twenty years before, who'd be daft enough to try it? it was usually worked by two hefty men.

I said it was steady downhill all the way to the Stage Door from the depot, I'd manage. (I never ever heard of anyone in stage management discuss *returning* props.) 'All right then,' said the Parks Manager, 'just don't get in front of it that's all, steer it from behind.' Heads rose from shrubberies and the distant putting green to watch me depart; park keeper called to park keeper in the hazy distance; it was like the Sioux Indians watching Custer ride into the Black Hills. The crunch and rumble of the two sections of the roller obliterated sound, but out of the corner of my eye I glimpsed grinning mouths shouting encouragement, or possibly satire.

I'd come to love stage effects and machines, the thundersheet (a large flexible sheet of metal with a thick rope handle by which you shake it to call up the *Götterdämmerung*); the doorslam (a sturdy wooden frame . . like a crate with no side-panels . . with a heavy wooden door at the top, which had various types of latches or knobs to lift it up and let it go to give a convincing sound of offstage arrival or departure . . . Nora's escape from the silk chains of her marriage at the end of *A Doll's House* is symbolized by just such a device), and the wind machine (a ribbed wooden drum set in a stout trestle, and a wide canvas strip which you hold down as you rotate the drum against it to give out with wuthering heights), all far far better than any effects record, where the sound comes out of speakers, rather than out of the surrounding air. The train effect was going to be the ultimate; the roller might well shake thick flakes of dried scene-paint from the waiting-room walls, but by the gods, the Ghost Train would go by.

I came out of the park gates. The traffic was sparse, so I didn't lose momentum as I crossed the wide road and set off down the gently sloping avenue leading to the city centre. Exhilaration filled my lungs under the enclosing trees that lined the way, this was the effortless progress of mounted knights in clattering armour, leisurely and full of power. The roller was picking up speed. Remembering the Parks Manager's warning, I let the roller go past me, and took up the strain from behind as the avenue grew steeper. As my charge and I accelerated, I glanced down, wondering if I'd failed to notice some sort of a brake. What happened if they needed to park it on a hill? The tarmac was now racing under my feet, individual stones and pebbles indistinct, like the Severn Bore without the foam. What happened if I met a milk float, parked while the man delivered? What about the lights at the crossroads? The two sections of the roller allowed for a certain amount of steering, so I kept to the centre line. The noise would give fair warning to the elderly or infirm; the emotionally fragile would likely stay indoors till whatever it was had roared on by.

My ears were beginning to burn and my eyes streamed as I dug my heels down in a series of hops to slow up. I reached the main road and the traffic lights; they were blurred, but I could see they were at red, and cross traffic was beginning to move. A motor-bike shot ahead in the middle lane, and then wobbled wildly as the driver tried to crane to look back in a cacophony of horns and hastily applied brakes, all saluting this antic figure in flapping tweed jacket and corduroys, bounding springheeled behind the speeding monster, banging and grinding like a shunting yard as we entered the more expensive of Leicester's two main shopping streets. I couldn't tell if the shoppers on the wide footpath were stationary as they flashed by, but the stunned disbelief on the face a policeman etched itself fleetingly on my mind's eye. A van was parked outside Elton's Fine China, a man with a small tea-chest in his arms seemed to be in some static frenzy of indecision, making small jerky steps on the spot as he debated abandoning the tea-chest or the van or both, and at the last moment sprang out of the roller's path as I managed a shallow arc to miss the van.

I screeched round the corner into the market, and discovered what I'd not noticed before: the last few yards to the Stage Door were slightly uphill, not much, but enough to allow me to slow down before I skittled the first few stalls. As it came to rest, I was able to let go, and search out Ted to help me get the roller inside, when there was a detonation of shattering crockery from behind me: one of the reasons I'd been able to stop was that I'd unwittingly used the bric-à-brac lady's stall as a longstop.

Emotionally, as well as physically exhausted, I gasped out grovelling apologies as I helped her reassemble her display . . it was a humiliating end to a wild and frightening runaway success. 'S'all seconds anyway,' she said, her voice quiet and unmodulated as ever, 'never had so many punters round in all the years.' I looked up, and there were people shoulder to shoulder, pushing forward, picking up miraculously unbroken tureens . . 'Be all right for flowers that, certainly a very solid piece a' pot.' Others loitered on the outside of the ruck to admire the destruction and ask what show was the roller for? Second absolute of theatre: whatever draws a crowd is good news, especially a disaster.

At the age of twenty-two, I was becoming aware of watching me watching; I was a one-man spectator sport. The devices of drama absorbed me because I had little outside life, no time for it, and because their use and effect filled out the emptiness within, let me into an understanding of others, gave me a place in a recognizable order of things. There was a strong, but rarely remarked sense of continuity in the company; as a poet accumulates impressions and images, and shapes them to a theme, so the films and popular icons of the early fifties were shadowed-out on those boards: Ray Milland, Bogart, Sydney Greenstreet, Lauren Bacall, Ingrid Bergman, Greer Garson, etc. appeared twice-nightly in Leicester.

It's doubtful if the audience noticed, or cared about the impersonations, they were simply part of the social climate; but they did give the actors confidence, a frame for their work, they were short cuts in a busy life.

Ray, however, was different, the unbroken line of his continuity went directly back into history, no short cuts. He'd started early in the business, sixteen, just after the war, at the time young men were being called up for National Service at eighteen; if your voice had broken, you were in. He became feed for an old character actor who played the music hall circuit, bringing down the first half, to the sound of tip-up seats tipping up, with Gems from Shakespeare; the second half was spent in the pub where the young apprentice absorbed the lore of fifty years and more of theatre and a taste for draught Guinness.

The old man had had a spell at Stratford-on-Avon with a legendary actor-manager, and told of how the boss's rotund diction, flamboyant gestures and raffish ways convinced the Theatre Board that maybe some more suitable, more respectable member of the company should read the lesson for the Shakespeare's Birthday Service. The boss was outraged at the slight, and boycotted the Service. As the company and the burghers of Stratford filed sedately out of the parish church, the Artistic Director stood, pint in hand, on the raised front rampart of the Black Swan, haranguing passers-by. One hand stretched trembling before him, head cast back in noble grief like Antony communing with slaughtered Caesar, he declaimed 'Give me one good rea-son, adduce me one cogent rea-son, why *I* should not read the fucking lesson!'

There were small ways in which Ray embodied an unquestioned tradition, for instance if he played a silly-ass part, which he often did, he painted a grey dot on each eyelid. When I asked him why he did it, Ray was bewildered, and finally confessed he didn't know why he did it, but that's what he always did. I saw it, in my innocence, as being something like the clown's makeup, patented and particular to each artiste, only in this case the makeup belonged to the part, not the performer. Then some chance took me out front during a performance, and I saw what the dots did: they gave Ray a double-blink, so that when he, and the audience with him, were contemplating some outrageous turn of the plot, his eyes flickered doubly with apprehension, which the audience shared with ecstasy.

However, around this time, English cinema and theatre audiences were beginning to experience the work of the New York Actors Studio, where the naturalistic explorations of Stanislavski were being applied to the many-layered American experience. As the Moscow Art Theatre briefly superseded the grand, operatic style of old Imperial Russian theatre, so the mannered superficiality the Americans inherited from European actors was being undermined and revivified by raw reporting from the street, and a ruthless exploration of the artiste's inner emotional life. It was no less mannered, as it turned out, than the old actor-manager expostulating from the front of the Mucky Duck, nor did it reveal any greater human truths, but the new style was meshed with the new drama, there was no place for little grey dots in *On the Waterfront*.

Then Ray was cast to play a young theatre director who takes on a one-time star now demolished by drink, his old-style barnstorming extravagance surplus to requirements in the modern dispensation. In the course of the play, the old lion reverts to type, and raises the scalp of all with a rumble of thunder from his distant youth, but it did need Ray's character to establish the edgy streetwise aggression, the raw naturalism against which the veteran actor-laddie must be seen. And he couldn't get near it. Ray was a comic performer, his own character had never been seen on stage. His accent was impeccable; his grasp of the plot, the young and ambitious director locked in a struggle for the talent of the drowning star, was complete . . though this wasn't surprising, the hectic pace of learning a script in two and a half days every week often meant that the plot was all the actor could hang on to; what he couldn't get was the abrasive attack, the sweat and the mumble.

The Director had asked Ted to make two large rostrums, which Gwyn was to paint a neutral grey, for the setting. This was to do with another current fashion, called 'power-grouping'; characters would stand higher or lower, according to their dominance or subservience in any given scene. It didn't seem to marry too well with the play's theme, but I was unshakeable in my faith in the Director, and had to suppose that such blatant artifice would enhance by contrast the grubby naturalism of the action. Ted could be heard daily sawing in ostentatious and bitter rage beneath the stage when he could have been in the pub. It outraged his sense of pride in craftsmanship that he should be required to construct a sturdy rostrum, only to see the bloody thing painted like a pissing camouflaged clapped-out battle cruiser. The atmosphere was not good, and I brooded on a line I'd found in the script where a character gazes out into the auditorium for a long, poignant moment, and then says 'Nothing quite so strange as a quiet and empty theatre.'

As I went about my prop-check after the morning's rehearsal, I became aware that the working lights were on onstage. It was inconceivable that rehearsals could go on into the afternoon, the human constitution wasn't capable of such a work-load, and yet, as I peered cautiously from the wings, there sat the Director in his rehearsal kit: wide black felt hat, camel-hair coat over his shoulders like Broderick Crawford, script in hand, taking Ray patiently through the role, reading out the line, feeding in the other characters, like a psychiatrist quietly talking a patient through trauma. Suddenly, as I watched from the shadows, the Director hurled the script to the floor, leapt to his feet, and jabbed out a finger at Ray, screaming out what I recognized to be an improvisation of Ray's speech where he blows away the ex-star's lies and evasions, and exposes the man to himself in all his hollowness. Ray was a stocky powerful young man, who often got into brawls in his few off-duty moments; the Director was slim, slope-shouldered, delicately framed; the scene was weird, yet oddly convincing: power-grouping without the rostrums. Ray, who would normally have decked any man that attacked him so violently, seemed lost, shifty. The murmured colloquy resumed, and after a few moments, I went to the Green Room; there were glasses to polish, whisky bottles to be topped up with cold tea.

Cigarettes were a problem. I had a cash float to buy them for a show, and the numbers to be smoked on stage were carefully logged by Reg from the prompt script. If they were left in the Prop Room, the actors would pinch them, so I had to count out an exact number to the actor immediately before the show, or put them into a cigarette box onstage: no actor would meddle with the props from when the half was called till curtain down, it seemed to be in the genes; at all other times, the law of the thieves' bazaar obtained, at least as far as cigarettes were concerned.

'Where you like dear, where you like,' intoned the bric-à-brac lady into the quiet afternoon. Ted's sawing fell away to silence, and the Stage Door slammed behind him as he went to catch Last Orders at the Swan.

Suddenly the peace of the afternoon was ripped apart by mayhem from the stage, Ray was barking like a demented dog. I darted to the wings again. The Director was backing round the stage, one arm up to protect himself from a barrage of vituperation, Ray was following him, jabbing out a finger on a fist clenched like a punch, grinding out almost meaningless words between teeth bared in paranoid rage, and the Director, hysterical, gasped interjections, 'Ray! that's it! Enough now Ray, you've got it!' It was as if Ray had gone berserk, shaking, and bloated with anger, and yet I noticed that in all the apparently uncontrolled frenzy, they neither of them left the confines of the acting area, chalked out for the morning's rehearsal in the current show's set; I was looking at an enclosed happening. Finally, the two petered out into an exhausted calm. They sat down.

Then Ray raised his right hand, index finger extended, gazing at it as if it were foreign to him; he jabbed it out experimentally a couple of times, and inspected it again. Mutely, the Director demonstrated with his own hand, and I could see at once that this gesture was balletic, it had shape, the finger described a small circle in the air, and came to rest posed, rather than poised; when the pointing finger stopped, the gesture was complete, the eye didn't follow a line indicated, as it did with Ray's new-learnt gesture. The very jabbing finger that Ray would stab into an opponent's chest before punches took over, he'd had to be taught to use it onstage, how to make an unfinished gesture. A world of meaning in a grain of sand.

The Leicester audiences were probably not ready for the new Ray, or his interpretation of Method Acting. They'd come to expect open-ended performances from him, where there was room for them as well. During one of the rough North Country comedies the company often presented, he'd been stuck on stage when Pam was off ('Sorry darling, I was on the loo'). The audience rapidly realized something was amiss when Ray opened a cupboard door, and shouted 'Help!' into the darkness within. Then he picked up a large prop cucumber which was inexplicably making up the number in a bowl of fruit . . The sudden clatter and shuffle as I left the Prompt Corner to find Pam further alerted the house, and Ray's comment 'Big mice' confirmed their eager expectations.

Nobody, including Ray and his audience, could remember exactly afterwards what he did with his cucumber during that aching hiatus, but by the time I had located Pam and hustled her down to the stage, he was doing trick snooker shots with invisible balls. She finally made her entrance, and gasped out her line. Ray rallied, registered the cucumber in his hand, returned it to the fruit bowl with the air of a man who wouldn't stoop to anything vulgar, and certainly wouldn't explain how he came to have it in his hand in the first place, carried on with the scene, looked back at the cucumber as if it had just landed from outer space, and rallied again. The play was crudish, but some special zest was added this particular night: Pam had her skirt tucked into her knickers at the back. When Ray spotted her ruched rump, and spun to see if the cucumber had somehow moved on its own to sabotage Pam's dignity, the audience may not have had the faintest idea what it was they so relished, but they relished it heartily. Third absolute of theatre, the Rule of Three, or, as Ray put it, 'Tell 'em you're going to tell 'em; tell 'em' and tell 'em you've told 'em.' The cucumber had become Punch's ribald and magical wand.

For his role as the American director, Frank lent Ray a beige tropical-weight jacket, which he said was near enough uniform in those circles, he'd seen photographs, and it was worn with a T-shirt. Ray didn't have a T-shirt, but he did have a low-necked canary yellow cotton pullover. The trousers weren't altogether authentic either, grey flannel, with generous English pleats at the waist, and turnups, but Frank reassured him that some Americans were still wearing peg-tops. The heavy, thick-soled brown brogues were all Ray had besides his black patent-leather evening shoes, so there was no discussion of footwear, except for Ted, who said if they were looking at your boots, you were in trouble already.

Ray's unusually big Adam's apple wasn't immediately seen to be working against his interpretation, but it did occur to me at the Dress that there was more of George Formby about it than Lee J. Cobb. First house Monday was watched with sullen respect, the applause cool, but as the Director said between houses, they were mostly comps anyway. In rehearsal, he'd proposed a certain casual ease in movement, even in the midst of emotional turmoil. He'd been on a short visit to New York, and had been fascinated by the way a cabbie's hand would hang limp out of the window during a heatwave, while the man cursed another driver in the most spectacularly foul language. However, he mused, in view of the stolidity of the Leicester first night audience, maybe they should move it along a bit second house, pick up the cues earlier, even overlap. That's what Marlon Brando did, after all, in *On the Waterfront*.

Since the actors didn't remember the cues too clearly anyway, overlapping was no problem, and they steamed into second house like the *Ghost Train* roller. Act One went by in a blur. When Ray came galumphing on in his brogues, the jacket flapping round him, he looked a bit like a blond Groucho Marx without the cigar, but this was no more than his audience expected of him; they just didn't seem greatly taken with the bits in between.

Although the text is in two acts, the Front of House Manager had insisted on the usual three, for the bar sales. This gave a baffling lumpishness to the story, with quite humdrum lines doing service as curtain lines. It wasn't so noticeable in rehearsal; it could be seen by the hopeful as part of the arbitrary slice-of-life nature of the piece. Taken at the new runaway pace, it had the audience in a tangible state of anxious tension.

Came the line 'Nothing quite so strange . .' (Act Two as played), Ray forgot the long poignant look out into the auditorium until half way through the line. He paused, flicked a glance out front, then back for '. . . as an empty and silent theatre'. The audience perked up, here at last was something they understood, Ray's double-take. A loyal fan snorted down his nose in joyous anticipation. Ray's Adam's apple bobbed up and down in profile. He swivelled again, fixed the offender with an aggrieved stare, then back to the scene in hand. The fan's guffaw detonated, then rippled through the audience like shock waves as Ray turned out front the third time, and jabbed out a finger at his happy admirer that would have harpooned the Great White Whale. Show-stopping laugh, if played correctly.

After the final curtain, Ray paused only to hang up Frank's jacket before disappearing into the night with a mutter of 'Don't want to get blood on it . .' I had little to do after the show, you can hardly tidy up three large grey rostrums, so I was hard on Ray's heels going into the Swan. The fan was there already, arms wide to welcome his idol. Ray stomped past him to the bar, turned as the man turned, and decked him. I caught the fan by the armpits as he dropped. 'Tell Ray there's a pint of draught Guinness on the bar for him,' the man said, 'make sure he drinks it before Cyril throws him out.'

5

Once more into the whirligig of time, with knobs on

Ray was sacked after the incident in the Swan. My life was filling up with absences. In Ray's presence, I'd felt to be connected to the company of raffish, vibrant ghosts, mummers all, from Epidaurus, by way of the gaudy crowded carts of the old Mystery Players, on trestles, in teeming inn-yards and noisy playhouses, planks and passions. I was in freefall now, and, like a parachutist, I could as well have been rising as falling, there was no sense any more of up or down. The only force that acted on me was gravity, in both senses of the word, I knew that. Whatever it was, it was serious, and when I came down to earth, it was going to be hard.

There was a mild fuss in the press over Ray's departure, but the fan's loyalty was undented. ' "Ray is an artiste," says theatregoer as he bathes his black eye. "They all have their temperaments. I shall continue to patronize the Theatre Royal." '

I was coming up to fifty-two weeks in the business, and could apply to join Equity. Frank gave me the address, and also the name of a restaurant in London, where I could get casual work between jobs. It took me some time to see the connection between the two pieces of information.

There were others from whom I could pick up hints about the trade. Bill, who'd had a mild stroke, and tried to build a pipe into every character, so that the slight distortion of his mouth would be disguised. Bill learned his part on the bus to and from the theatre, so it was all a bit sketchy. He'd been in twice-weekly at an early point in his career. 'We started off with *The Silver King*, and did a different play twice a week. But it was always *The Silver King*,' he told me. On the book, I noticed that Bill could grope his way through largely by his tenacious grip on the plot, as a child clings to your finger with primitive power. I also noticed that he knew the play a lot better on Friday than he ever did on the Monday; but he never dried, it was the others I had to prompt, when they were thrown by the bum cues he gave them.

Sheri, the Leading Juvenile Lady, gave me a more professional clue to the art of study. She had long shapely legs, huge dark eyes spaced and thickened by hot-black mascara that batted her myopic glances to every seat in the house like a pair of Aldis lamps. We sat together in the De Montfort Gardens on a fresh summer afternoon. She would read a sentence, cover it up, and say it, look again, repeat it, read the next sentence, cover it up, and so on. When she'd done this for a full page, she handed me the book, and I cued her in. It took her about two minutes to learn a page, solid and unshakeable. The afternoon was made more torrid by her habit of touching my knee or my hand lightly to get my attention when she wanted to be heard. After half an hour she had my total attention, and I had a masterful hard-on.

I was beginning to wonder if I'd ever blink again, when she kissed me on the cheek, rose on her teetering high heels, and sailed off to her digs for tea. I sat there still on the bench, gave her what I hoped was a worldly and debonair wave, and folded my hands on my lap, pulling up the skirts of my jacket over the tumult in my loins. I knew that her seductive gaze, her grace and playful gestures were routine, part of her actress toolkit, because she did it with everyone, but it worked on me all the same. Fourth absolute of theatre: the director, the leading players, may find they have things in common; the juveniles may well share the teeming joys of youth; but the ASM had better make friends with the five-fingered widow.

Before Ray was replaced, I got the odd small part, so Sheri's other lesson was useful: what with emptying the dustbin, collecting props, prompting, scene setting and striking, making the calls front of house and backstage and making tea, I needed to be a quick study. Reg taught me makeup. A basic undercoat of Leichner's No.5 (putty-coloured), then No.9 (brick-coloured) as a blusher on the cheekbones, point of the chin and the brow. Then the eyes, a very fine white line (No.20) painted round the inside of the lashes with a tiny brush greased with Trex cooking fat (also used for removing greasepaint), red dots at the inner corner of each eye, and green (II) faintly over the eyes. Reg insisted on Green II, not I or III, and complained that I was using the wrong one every time I got a part. Certainly, in the dim light of the Stage Management dressing-room, I looked to myself like a menswear dummy in a downmarket tailor's window. It didn't occur to either of us that Reg was red-haired, with green eyes and a high complexion, whereas I was dark, pale and had grey eyes. We both accepted that makeup was a fixed convention, and that I was a gawky young clown.

Reg also taught me gag-timing. 'You're throwing away a good laugh, it's gag-timing,' he snarled after first and then second house on the Monday. Come Tuesday, Reg was explosive. The exchange went . . .

> PAM: Our Jeremy's been summonsed.
> ME: He's starting young, what for?

The underlying information being that the said Jeremy had been called to an audition at the BBC, and Pam, as his mother, hadn't got it quite right. 'It's gag-timing, *gag-timing*,' snapped Reg, tears of exasperated frustration standing in his eyes at the first interval, his hands spread before him, palms out as if demanding the return of a long-borrowed umbrella.

'Is that faster? slower? leave a pause?'

'Gag-timing for heaven's sake!'

'You do it for me,' I said. I delivered Pam's feed line as best I could:

> ME: Our Jeremy's been summonsed.
> REG: (crisp on cue) He's starting *young*; what *for*?

Reg had the advantage of a Welsh background for the rising intonation of the last phrase, but there's a bit of the Celt in most English people, and this simple mechanism astounded me, to the extent that it became impossible for me to get it wrong. There were even moments when I got a laugh where no laugh was, an unnerving error which threw my fellow actors, and gave me the feeling that a dog seems to have when it farts, and then spins round to find out where the noise came from.

I'd just finished bucketing out the dustbin, and was on my way back down to stage level, when I heard violent voices from below. It was as if the market had invaded the theatre, authentically raucous and vulgar. The management making its monthly raid. Husband and wife, both laden with gold rings, both grizzled, they arrived every four weeks with a large battered skip. Curtains, chair-covers, rugs, whatever had lost its novelty at their other two theatres, all as mucky and dust-laden as when they were thrown into the skip. It crossed my mind, as I hurried down the four flights of stairs towards the racket, that if such a couple were to be represented in art of any kind, from a painting to Grand Opera, in anything like their true colour and vigour, it would come over as parody, impossibly exaggerated.

The company always seemed to find urgent business elsewhere, including and probably especially Ted, as soon as their arrival was detected. Madam was hauling the skip up the stairs from the Stage Door, her husband waited at the top.

'You're about as much use as a chocolate teapot,' she roared up at him.

'You bleeding know I've got this bleeding bad bleeding heart,' he bellowed back, 'where is everybody? Get 'em on that bleeding tannoy!'

I made to go to the Prompt Corner, quite glad to rest my eardrums. Madam stopped me with a screech like rending sheet metal. 'Bleeding cop 'old of the other end of this bleeding skip, damn you!' There didn't seem to be much malice in their vociferations, but I wondered how they talked to each other at home. I gripped the top handle of the skip as she sweated and panted loudly down to the other end below. 'Men, I'd rather have a cucumber sandwich,' she gasped, like a hippopotamus breaching.

Gwyn and Alex, the Director, and Reg arrived, and stood about looking shifty and dispirited before she'd even flung back the lid. It was bad enough having to look upon these shabby faded cast-offs, without Madam treating them as if they were Tutankhamun's treasure. She lifted out a set of chair-covers, and long curtains that seemed vaguely related if only in the uniformity of their faded shabbiness, and draped them about the Green Room, 'Just short of a bit of ironing,' she gasped at full volume as she dived back in for the next goody. Her husband fingered his wig as if in the presence of royalty, clearly convinced that the next revelation was going to impress. The company was beginning to gather, sheepish, outside the door, peering in.

'You're going to see something now,' bawled the boss at them. Alex tried to deflect his employers' enthusiasm for the fifth-hand: 'I was thinking we might do *Murder in the Cathedral*,' he said. Any discussion of play policy usually quietened them for a bit.

'There you are then,' yelled Madam, head down in the skip. 'Them Art Deco drapes is just right for a thriller.'

The prize exhibit was hauled out and thrown about the room for all to see and marvel at: a job lot of remaindered Shakespearean costumes from some justifiably bankrupted touring company. Gwyn hastily took the ones that hit him into the Prop Room next door, his head averted, and breathing through his mouth to avoid the foul dust and stale stench of the glorious past and old sweat.

Reg liked frocks and took more interest. 'Look,' he said, showing Gwyn the label inside a threadbare doublet, 'Alec Guinness. I wonder what she wore that for?'

'Oooh look, here's another one,' said Gwyn.

'Is there? My heavens, whose was that?'

'Grimaldi,' said Gwyn.

Their employers had gone, taking last month's leavings with them for recycling with the other companies, so the satire was more or less wasted. But Alex was looking thoughtful.

'I wonder how many of us would be interested in fencing?' he said. I could see a vague connection between the ageing period costumes and the Director's remark, but Alex's face was a mask. He couldn't really be thinking of putting on a Shakespeare, could he? Even with realistic duels, and plenty of blood, it didn't somehow fit with the image the company had established. The prospect of learning a Shakespeare text in a week, even with the Thursday off to learn it, and employing Sheri's formidable technique, was daunting. As Frank said, 'They don't half *talk*, don't they?' However, I concluded that whatever transpired, at least I would extend and deepen my apprenticeship. I was to be proved painfully right.

I'd discovered early that the things I found out for myself were invariably the most valuable. From primary school to university, I'd dodged the curriculum as much as I could, and applied myself to any book that wasn't on it. I'd discovered John Skelton, the rampageous Tudor poet, and devoured him in preference to Wordsworth or any other dense and worthy on the set book list.

I'd a good short-term memory, and coasted through exams on a cursory reading of the official texts and their footnotes, and forgot them at once.

So, to prepare myself for fencing, and whatever might lie beyond, I got myself a book. *The Art of Fencing.* And I brushed up on my judo falls. I reckoned I'd better be able to fall spectacularly; at this stage in my career I couldn't see myself being cast as the winner. Nor was I, at any point in my career. Judo falls are directional; you can choose which way you're going to land, even in mid-air, you just choose which shoulder to roll over. Ray's pratfalls had been an impenetrable mystery to me; they were so seemingly unexpected, and looked so painful, I couldn't figure why he didn't cripple himself twice-nightly.

Much later, playing King Rat in pantomime, I had to be slaughtered by a team of cats, under Puss's command. In this show, the murderous cats were a team of tumblers, and there again I saw Ray's way of doing it, the ancient arts of the circus. After a week of it, I had a raw and bleeding bruise on my hip-bone, and try as I might, I couldn't avoid grinding on it again every performance. The falls I'd learnt from my book were designed to distribute the impact over the whole body, so the hip had to have it, every time.

In the end, I had to go to the leading tumbler, and beg him to ask the boys to vary their way of tossing me in death, and I showed him my wound. 'That's no good,' said Johnny, 'you don't want that eh? We're always getting them.' He reached into a large pillow-case under his dressing-room table, and pulled out a lump of sorbo rubber. 'Get some lint round that,' said Johnny, 'and stuff it into your jockstrap. Soon clear up. I never pass a wrecked-car lot without vandalizing the upholstery a bit.'

Ray's pratfalls were every bit as painful as they looked. I marvelled again.

In so far as anything could become established, except the iron wheel of getting plays on and off, fencing sessions became a regular date, half an hour before rehearsals, Tuesdays and Fridays. Pam was a bit stately about it, but most of the men grew leaner and fitter and more stylish. Sheri took no part, and anyway without high heels she looked vaguely diminished. Then Alex let slip his hidden agenda: he'd persuaded the management we could do *Cyrano de Bergerac*, and what's more, not only would he direct, but he would also play Cyrano himself. The company was dumbfounded. Alex's light, slightly nasal voice and spindly frame were ideal for comedy; the rugged pugnacious golden-voiced Gascon soldier of fortune didn't seem obvious casting for him, even to me, who held the Director in awe and reverence.

Alex was a thesaurus of sight-gags. To see him directing knockabout, raising his wide black felt hat with both hands as each new impeccably logical lunacy came to him, turning it full circle and then ramming it down on his gleeful head, his grey eyes alight, a small V-shaped smile of impure delight on his lips, was like watching a fireworks display of anarchy. But in *tights*? It also came to me that for the past month, I'd been auditioning for the part of the bold swordsman that Cyrano fights while composing a sonnet, and who gets skewered on the last line of the *envoi*. Not only a part, but a death to boot. I redoubled my studies of my *Art of Fencing* book, especially the sabre part, which I considered would make for more spectacular effects, slashing and lunging, and the ring of steel on steel. Oh yes, I'd show Leicester that Errol Flynn wasn't the only one who could swash and buckle.

Most of the company were a bit subdued at rehearsals. It tended to look a bit doomed, over-ambitious, to them, and they had plenty of time to look: Cyrano and the two lovers do most of the talking. Sherri's dashing and quintessentially modern good looks and brittle West End delivery were not altogether useful as the passionately docile Roxane, courted by proxy, and ending her virtuous days in a nunnery. She suspected her charming buck teeth, with the sexy gap in the middle, were going to look perverse in a wimple. Reg, on the other hand, was acutely happy as the poetic pastrycook, whose shop is the setting for the big duel. He borrowed my long chef's apron from Bell Hotel days, and bleached and starched it till it rattled. He somehow found a voluminous pastrycook's hat, which flapped flamboyantly as he flounced about, and the matinee-idol makeup, mascara for his ginger eyelashes, green eye-shadow (Leichner No. II), took him a concentrated forty minutes, especially if he had a friend out front.

I told Alex I'd read up on judo falls, then wished I hadn't. 'Great,' said Alex, 'I'll kill you on the balcony, and you can do a backwards fall off it; I'll show you how later.'

I had a poor head for heights, and while I had a groundplan to chalk out the stage for rehearsal, I didn't know about the elevation. Why on earth hadn't I paid proper attention to the script? There *had* to be a balcony, there was a balcony *scene* for heaven's sake. I went to see

Ted. 'Twelve foot,' said Ted, 'and he wants it reinforcing with scaffolding for some pigging reason he hasn't bothered to tell me. It's going to be a pigging death-trap, whatever I stiffen it with. I only hope he's got no one going up on it, except Sheri in the balcony scene, and she's no weight. I've told her not to jump about too much.'

Outwardly, it was a quiet and peaceful afternoon. I sat in the Green Room, a sandwich balanced on the arm of the chair, a sheet of newspaper on the floor before me, a small pot of black enamel paint, with fine brush, and four fencing sabres, to which I'd fitted round foil guards, which last I was painting with curlicues to give them a period aspect, as if they were made of chased silver. Through the open door I could see backstage, the white arrows of sunlight through the cracks of the elephant doors, and Gwyn on his paint frame, painting the shadows on the caryatids. His brush made faint scuffing noises on the canvas as he worked. The bric-à-brac lady outside the Stage Door called her tranquil call into the afternoon, 'Where you like dear, where you like . .' The actors had long gone to their digs, or the pub. Inside me, there was a still, cold foreboding.

Ted's scaffolding was already assembled, though not yet cladded or anchored. It stood in the gloom of backstage, looming, waiting, Dr Guillotine's engine of death, patent applied for. I went to have a look. The lighting board was above the Prompt Corner, access by a vertical steel ladder. Twelve feet. In flurried moments of concentration, I could imagine it to be a near-replica of the balcony to come. I struggled to remember the many film scenes where the actor negotiates a fall from some parapet, and realized soon that the cutting-room was probably more important there than the skill of the stunt man. The scenes seemed jerky in my recollection, jumping from perspective to perspective. I longed for a cut to 'Many weeks later . . .' I forced myself to go for a closer look. Well, it seemed possible. If I keeled over backwards, gripping the rail behind me, and waited till my arms were at full stretch before letting go, the actual freefall would be less than six feet, then the backwards roll as I hit the floor.

It began to look almost likely, it could even be quite impressive. I mounted the steel rungs with the composure of an unjustly condemned man. Right. Right. Cyrano's imaginary blade apparently enters ghastly cad's ribcage, actually under upstage armpit, is tugged out (must remember to ask for blade to be clear of legs as I go over), perhaps Cyrano salutes a brave foe, good that, distracts audience's attention from corpse gripping rail behind his back (ask for balcony rail to be clear of cladding at that point). Right.

The lighting board and the fly gallery revolved over me at a slowly accelerating nightmare pace, arms reach full stretch, decelerate the fall, then twang like a Roman siege catapult, back and then forward, the whole scaffold rocking in a powerful convulsion, I felt, rather than heard the uprights thud back to the stage floor again as I arc'd through the air to thud down full length on my face, no trace of a backwards roll, ambition gone for ever, wondering if my breath would ever come back again. I lay there for a moment or two, thoughtless and dateless, then hoisted myself to my feet, and limped back towards the Green Room.

As I passed the paint frame, Gwyn suddenly spun round and gave a galvanic yelp, 'Good grief what was *that*?'

I looked up, unable yet to speak.

'There was a most terrible thump.'

I shook my head helplessly, 'Didn't hear a thing,' I gasped finally, and went back to painting curlicues with trembling hands. 'Where you like dear, where you like . . .'

Then my father died. He'd retired early from the tyre and tube industry to which he'd contentedly given his working life, discouraged at last by the rapacity of Directors and Board, who, like my bosses, would invest little, and extract ever-increasing profits. Crumbling workshops were demolished, the sites laid out for car-parks, while machines were crowded ever more dangerously into the surviving buildings. While Britain boomed with reconstruction and full employment, management seeded carelessly or not at all. Also he had a minor heart complaint, probably as a result of working too hard and too long hours during the height of the war. No overtime for the man in the suit, nothing to show for it except a war won and a poorly heart.

His death was no surprise, but it devastated my mother. Since they'd retired to the Leicester countryside, I was able to give up my digs in town, and stay with her for a while. She could have been a girl of seventeen as she looked out into the little orchard, where the new leaves, creased in birth, unfolded as the morning mist lifted, the fresh-dug loamy vegetable-beds her husband had left. 'Oooh I shall miss him,' she said. No tears, just a sweet gust of passion. At fifty-five.

Young as I was, I was not well acquainted with death, but I could understand this bit. What little I knew of my parents was that their relationship had been strongly sensual. As a child of nine, rooting in their bedroom, I'd come across the dark green rubber contraceptive douche hidden there among musty spare sheets. The teachings of Marie Stopes in the book on the top of the wardrobe were a mystery, but the diagrams in the booklet for the douche were clear enough, as were the sighs and cries of joy in the night.

My father left very little of himself. A couple of old pipes he'd long given up smoking. The broken-backed photo album, like so many, recorded early marriage, my own and my sister's childhood, and then petered out in holiday snaps, views, and sunsets when colour film came in. Since my father took most of the pictures, there were only a handful of him, usually looking vaguely anxious that his wife wouldn't get it right. I found the rickety old shotgun, greased it, and hid it among fluff under the spare-room bed, where I knew my mother would be unlikely to look. If she found it, she'd give it away. She loathed it, although she was pleased enough to get the occasional rabbit, or brace of pigeons her husband brought in from the fields and copses.

If I ever got any time to myself, I planned to teach myself to use the gun, from a book. My father wouldn't ever let me near it; no one knew when he was using it, he slipped off without a word, and reappeared a couple of hours later with the bag. For all my mother knew, he was working at the far end of the garden, and she probably preferred it that way. For one thing, her husband was too quietly bolshie to get himself a licence. I came across the cartridges when I was putting some peelings in the dustbin, and retrieved them, as silent on the subject as my father had been. It was disconcerting to find how much like the man I didn't know I was becoming; the plodding walk, the slight stoop, even the high-pitched morning farts. Was it possible I'd inherited the low expectations as well?

I'd started to write, on my mother's old typewriter. She was politically active, and was Minute Secretary for the 1946 Pan Africa Conference in Manchester. I used her paper and carbons. A short play in verse after the manner of Christopher Fry. I didn't like it, and wondered why. Perhaps the world of jewelled and playful words, with opulent and exquisite sets, usually by Oliver Messel, which so delighted West End audiences and the provincial Number One touring dates, after the greyness of war and peacetime austerity, was what I *didn't* want. Life was already valuable, was that it? It didn't need jewellery to make it acceptable? I didn't spend much time on the subject, just junked my script, and tapped on blindly into the future.

Then I sold a poem to the BBC – in Birmingham – so it was probably because I had a Midlands address. I didn't care, six guineas was nearly twice what I got at the Theatre Royal for seventy hours or more a week, and I didn't have to go to the Front Office to collect. I gloated over the cheque all the way to work on the bus. It was a half-hour journey, and I gloated very vigorously, so it was quite grubby before I got it to the Box Office. 'Could you change that into money for me?' I said, 'I want to see what it looks like.'

I took Ted for a couple of pints in the Swan to celebrate, and also to enquire about the balcony, how firmly was it going to be anchored? Ted said why was I so piggin' interested in that monstrosity, and I told him. After a minute or two of polite exchanges, during which Ted burbled into his beer every so often, and blew his nose quite a lot, he disappeared into the Tap Room, said he had a man to see about some business. People started coming across to the hatchway, and looking across at me as I sat waiting for my friend to return, and pausing as they passed on their way to the gents, to stare at me keenly for a moment, and then going away spluttering and squeaking. When Ted came back, he was wiping his eyes.

I thought I'd better have a word with the Director. I found him in conference with the Front of House Manager, a man never seen without his stained dinner jacket, richly starched dress shirt, moribund buttonhole and desiccated patent leather shoes. It turned out the current show had 'rung the bell'. This was a system whereby if the Box Office receipts went over a certain percentage, a bonus was added to the company's wages. I caught this, and thought perhaps things were really looking up. I told Alex that I'd tried the twelve-foot backwards fall, off the lighting bridge. 'Good,' said Alex, 'Ted's got the scaffold up, I'll get him to brace and weight it, and we'll try the routine out when we get to it tomorrow.' 'I think I may have broken a rib,' I said.

The Manager had the knobbly technicolour complexion of a whisky enthusiast, but he paled momentarily. 'Management can take no responsibility for actions taken by an employee on his own initiative,' he said. 'Might be better to do it off a table,' said Alex. 'I could do it head first off a table,' I said. 'To play as cast, and to accept all reasonable direction from the Theatre Management,' said the Manager, 'it's in the contract.' 'I haven't got a contract,' I said, 'if I had a contract, I'd be on eight pounds a week.' 'Quite so,' said the Manager, a faint sweat glistening on his forehead, 'excuse us.' There was the impersonal tone of dismissal in his voice.

As I passed round cups of tea and plates of ham sandwiches after the funeral, the assembled family bickering quietly round me ('You never seem to come round for a visit, I wish you would the odd time. Family's family.' 'Last time you said we had to be quiet for *The Archers*.' 'Slightly better than leaping up to clean the ashtray every time somebody strikes a match.'), I wondered whether I wanted to be remembered at all, if this was what it came down to. The rackety life I was living, the moments of wondrous clarity, when audience and performer merge into one, no matter how tawdry the context, the play, the theatre, these were as indestructible as they were fleeting. It was the very falsehood that made it true: 'It is true that we are enacting a lie.' Somewhere, somebody is doing Grock's act, in which the piano is too far from the stool, so he toils to move the concert grand nearer the stool. And after Herculean efforts, the stool ends up too close, so he has to play with his belly up against the keyboard. No person living has seen that act, and yet it lives.

Uncle Jack sat with his hat on, whistling tunelessly and quite loud. He was a newsagent and tobacconist whose black market trade in rationed sugar, butter and tea and such had left him with large bolster-slips stuffed with pound notes. Uncle Jack knew my mother despised him, so he sat staring before him, whistling, with his hat on. Next to Jack, his wife and partner in the business. Long straight neck, seamed by a crude thyroid operation in adolescence, hair punished by a bristly perm the colour of cigarette tobacco, bolt upright on the sofa, she looked as if she'd survived a botched attempt to hang her. Two lives, and a lifetime, side by side on a sofa, as much a summation of their own history and time as any actor dressed up for the Battle of Britain, more vivid than any painted king. Was this to be my purpose? To mirror my corner of the age from the low angle of a ragamuffin child? It didn't occur to me then, or at any time, that there might be a disparity between my jaunty hopes and my actual prospects.

Cyrano was a lot more successful than the company had feared. Sheri kept her lips closed over her front teeth as much as possible, I found the pain in my ribs quite bearable if I took an aspirin immediately before the show . . and it looked, even as early as second house Wednesday, likely that we'd ring the bell yet again. Even Bill was saying most of his lines. The bus journey to and from work made my schedule even more fraught, especially as more of the stage management fell to me while Reg concentrated on his makeup. Then Reg ran out of No.5, an anxious moment, as he had a very special friend out front. I was happy to lend him mine when I finally made it to the dim dressing-room. Reg was hogging the light and whimpering feverishly. I had conceived a notion to have a little painted moustache, curled up in a stylish twist. This, I thought, would give my appearance a little more dash as I swiftly applied the basics Reg had taught me, borrowing back the stick Reg had borrowed, then the new moustache, before donning the costume and hurtling back down to the Prompt Corner to call Beginners.

What I didn't know, and had to be told later, was that the stick I'd borrowed back so briefly was not No.5, but Reg's Chrome Yellow. It did seem a bit colourful, but I put it down to the rosy blush of hectic physical exertion. I powdered over it heavily (Woolworth's California Poppy), and finally redefined the shiny black strokes of the Ronald Colman moustache (Leichner No.12). Come the duel, there was nobody on the book, as both Reg and I were on stage. This didn't matter much, as Alex knew the sonnet solidly; and Pam was on stage too, and so wouldn't have to be rooted out of the loo.

I turned to make my fatal challenge, my voice cutting into the rhubarb round the gallant Cyrano, who stood, facing away, listening with nobly bowed head to the insult offered. He raised his head, turned slowly to face me. Alex had a fairly noble nose already, which might explain his otherwise inexplicable enthusiasm for the part, but he'd also added to it with plasticine. As Cyrano turned, the nose described a horizontal arc, stopped, did a little wobble, and then did another little wobble before setting off back again. And then turned back for another look. It was a good, still moment, I thought, summarizing Cyrano's gallantry and the tragedy of his deformity. However, the retort spirited didn't come, the nose shot back to face front. Reg muttered the line to Alex, but stopped when he registered my appearance. I couldn't believe my new moustache made all that much difference, and stood my ground, waiting for Alex to get back on track. Not knowing that the Chrome Yellow, plus the brick-red No. 9 put me in fair competition with a Tequila Sunrise, I wondered apprehensively if I wasn't witnessing the most emphatic triple-take in the whole of theatrical history, and if it was, what was it doing for anyone in *Cyrano de Bergerac*?

The audience, however, was well ahead of the story, and was waiting for the upstart mustachioed popinjay to get his come-uppance at the swordpoint of their weedy reed-voiced hero. If the upstart looked like an advanced case of yellow jaundice, all the more reason for his come-uppance. It was irrelevant to them that when the duel finally got under way, Cyrano kept his head averted, as if he were doing it by numbers, or that the pastrycook *patron*'s mouth lay open waiting for the strength to close it again. It all added to the dangerous tension of the confrontation. What mattered was that the baddie got his well-earned skewering, especially when he leapt onto the table to gain a caddish advantage. Fifth absolute of theatre: given half a chance, the audience knows the plot far better than any individual actor.

What with one thing and another, it was the following Thursday before I could get to Casualty. An X-ray confirmed that yes, I had broken a rib. The nurse who strapped me up with wide bands of Elastoplast said she hoped I hadn't been doing anything silly. I told her no, barring emptying a dustbin every time it rained, not since Saturday. I'd been falling head-first off a table twice-nightly mind, I said, but that was last week. 'We get all sorts of nutters in here,' she said, pursing her lips over her task, 'especially on a Saturday night.'

When I got back to the theatre, there was a message via Ted to go to the Front Office. 'Always write out your resignation before you go to see a theatre manager,' he said. 'Then if he sacks you, you thump it down in front of him, and tell him no he's not, you're sacking him. Doesn't do a piggin' bit of good, but you feel better. Your Equity card's come, it's in the letter rack,' Ted added. I wondered if the Manager had perhaps caught a glimpse of my performance as a Belisha beacon. The man didn't spend a lot of time in the auditorium; the bars, foyer and his office were his domains, in each of which he could calculate the money as it came in. The stage was where it went out.

'You seem to have plenty of leisure,' said the Manager. Detecting disapproval, possibly to do with makeup, I started to explain the crossed lines that had led up to it. 'I've ordered a fresh supply of dressing-room lights,' said the man, as if that were my fault too. 'You artists don't seem to understand what costume plays *cost*. We paid a bonus on *Cyrano*,' he said, 'it's all money.'

'Didn't we earn it?' I said.

'That's another thing, your attitude. We're going to have to terminate your contract.'

'It's time I was calling the half,' I said, 'I haven't got a contract.'

'That's what I mean about your attitude. You'd better learn that in theatre it doesn't do to keep sniping at management. You'll get yourself a reputation as a trouble-maker. And you've got pinholes in your trousers.' He took a bottle of whisky out of his desk drawer, set out two tumblers, and poured out a generous measure for both of us. 'Good health, and here's to your future,' he said, and downed his in one. We shook hands.

'If you boiled up that tuxedo of yours,' I said, 'you'd get a nourishing broth. Cheers.'

I sat on the London train, in my father's best and last fine tweed suit; my father's battered old leather suitcase on the rack above me; in my head, my father's locked-up silence. On the top of the few clothes and toiletries, I'd packed a photograph of the front portico of the Theatre Royal, which the company had all signed, with cheerful and encouraging messages. Miniaturized by the camera, the peeling stucco columns and façade looked very fine. I'd been astonished by the affectionate formality of the goodbyes. They'd gathered in the Green Room at the half, to present me with a fencing foil, and the photograph. To prepare such gifts, I realized, they must have known I was going well before I did.

During the last few benumbed days of my apprenticeship, I'd been mulling over my attitude. Try as I might, I couldn't detect even a faint outline of my own character, but there were some dimly remembered markers. Mr Cottrell, French master at the Grammar School had spotted a boy whose attention had been caught by something beyond the playground railings. The master followed the boy's gaze. It was a man sweeping up leaves. 'So, a man sweeping up leaves is of more interest than your studies, is he boy? You carry on like that boy, and that's what you'll be doing in a few years, sweeping up, and fit for nothing better.'

'It's my father,' said the boy.

Then there was my military service, where I'd rapidly

discovered that I could escape the mindless discipline by working nights in the cookhouse. It wasn't so much that I defied authority, more that I wasn't there to be told off to perform the daft duties, like polishing boots soaked in cookhouse grease, or buttons made of brass that became tarnished and then green on my best uniform as it hung unworn in the cupboard. 'Stand by your beds', the command I heard once a week from under rumpled bedclothes, while the rest of the billet stood to attention next to their neatly laid-out kit, never failed to remind me that I was spending two years in the company of lunatics.

On rare and reckless occasions, a service policeman had bawled me out, say, for not wearing my hat, or threatened me with a charge for coming back late off leave, but a mild interjection of 'Corporal, don't you *want* to eat?' usually calmed them down. Was that an 'attitude'? At the theatre, I'd thrown myself enthusiastically into the performance of the most peculiar of instructions, even when everyone else round me clearly saw that what I was doing was stir-crazy. Mind, I did throw away my Leichner Green No. II.

The clank and rattle of the Sunday train lulled me into a fitful doze, in which I saw myself in Grimaldi's greasy sweat-stained doublet, scurrying up strange unfamiliar back entries, having to explain myself to strangers who thought I was an intruder among the dustbins, a braggadocio with a painted moustache, who deserved to die, and did, with a mercifully brief but savage stab of pain in my ribcage, the audience applauding a story I knew they knew and I didn't. I forced my eyes open, blinking away the daymare. On my lap, my new book on clay pigeon marksmanship, an escape from unwelcome imaginings. I set myself to read.

I was fascinated to be told that we have a leading eye, and that you can find out which it is by pointing at an object with both eyes open, then closing one eye: if the object appears to move, then you've closed the leading eye, if the object stays where it is when you wink, then it's the eye that's open that leads. I tried it out the window, and found it was my right eye that held the point accurately, nor was the effect marred by the mucky window, or by the moving target. I turned round to the corridor side, and tried it on the Third Class sign outside, wink wink. The elderly gentleman with the leather pouch that I'd come across on that last sad London trip was gazing in at me.

He came into the carriage and sat down, benign as ever, not in the least alarmed by my manic winks. I realized with a start that I'd been in a sort of minor shock. My little world had crumbled round me, and I'd been unable to see what was going on. I started to explain my apparently insane behaviour, but the man held up a neat pale hand with a thick gold ring on the third finger, 'I prefer no explanation, nuh? The joy of theatre lies in its crystalline mystery.'

I wondered if there were still traces of makeup in the roots of my hairline, 'How did you know I was in theatre?'

'You have a strap round your suitcase to hold it closed.'

I looked up to the luggage rack in wonder, and then back again to the old man.

'Also my wife and I go to the Theatre Royal, first house Wednesday, every week.'

'I've been sacked,' I said.

The little man looked thoughtful, finally, 'I shall continue to patronize the Theatre Royal,' he said, 'though we shall miss your appearance.'

'Appearances,' I said, 'I was getting quite a few parts.'

'Appearance,' said the old man, 'it was intriguing to speculate on what colour you would be this week.'

6

Smiling Through

Gualterio was a tall, queenly young man who waited table with an indefinable air of someone who is used to something more exalted. I'd got a casual job washing up at the Bicyclette. I still had my cook's whites and knives, and rapidly graduated from the *plonge* to chef, working alongside Sebastien, a pale excitable young Frenchman, whose English came straight out the Princess's English lesson in *Henry V*. Gualterio's languid ways goaded Sebastien nightly to new flights of invective. 'Where is my numero seexteen?' he would call down the food lift, and Sebastien would hurl himself at the open shaft, crash whatever pan he happened to have in his hand into the hardboard wall above, and bellow up 'Ees in de bleddy leeft! You aire too bleddy lazee to pool it one other centimetre! You pool it OK if is you deek you bleddy fecking cown!' Regular customers would ask to be seated as near as possible to the voluble dumb-waiter.

I'd found a bedsit within walking distance of Euston, and therefore not too far from the Charing Cross Road, where many theatrical agents had their offices. The room was clean, had an ancient gas fire, and a one-ring electric cooker. The telephone was down by the front door, the trains to and from the North screeched and clanged and screamed like a satanic steel mill in the wide cutting far below at the back of the house. I was careless of my surroundings, but even I could see that it was macabre. The single centre light cast shadows rather than brightness; what colour the paint and wallpaper had ever had had been leeched out by the years rather than sunlight; the ancient carpet had pile only under the bed. But since the restaurant was way the other side of town in Victoria, I spent little time at home, arriving there on the all-night number 12 bus in the early hours. Also, I got one first-class meal every day except Monday, when the restaurant was closed.

Among many other tips, Frank had given me the name of an agent he knew, Beryl, whose tiny office was up two narrow flights of stairs just off the Charing Cross Road. I phoned, and was given an appointment. This was beginning to feel like show business, as described by Reg. You phoned, hoped the secretary that took the call didn't pass it on that you were using a call-box, said you'd just lately finished work in the Midlands (Orson Welles had said New York, and got himself a job at the Abbey Theatre on the strength of it, but I didn't think I'd get away with anything so impressive, not in my father's suit), and lo, you were launched. She even took me for a lunchtime drink at her club, I was feeling quite chipper. She was a small, handsome woman, whose firm and very female shape, and neat head of dark grizzled hair had a reined-in look. It was impossible to imagine Beryl mussed up. The Venus de Milo, I thought, would have looked like Beryl, if she'd had the use of her hands to tidy her toga.

She opened the street door on the bare wooden stairway leading down to the club, and a strong smell of Jeyes Fluid, stale beer, and cigarette smoke wafted up from below. 'The Iron Lung,' she said, 'sniff deep: that is the richly authenticated smell of failure.' She introduced me to a tall, pale young man with sandy curls, wearing a capacious buttonless herringbone tweed overcoat held together loosely with a belt. His whole persona seemed to be held together loosely, and his faintly Irish voice seemed to come and go in the hubbub of trained voices around us. This was Godfrey, gently knitting his gangling frame as he talked, and then unknitting it again. He had a plan to set up a short season of three plays at the Empire Belfast, and Beryl told him that if it suited, I would complete the company he'd asked her to assemble. It seemed it suited, even before I had told him of my vast experience, in fact Godfrey seemed mysteriously indifferent to what I'd done before, so I told him the scheme showed every sign of promising a success, and we shook hands on it. Four days out of work, and here I was in work again. Wow.

Godfrey had complimentary tickets for a show written by a friend, which was to open in a small club theatre in Notting Hill, would I like to go? At least one member of the new company would be there. Godfrey didn't explain why he wasn't going to root for his friend's play, but I was learning that Godfrey didn't explain much, though he did say it was about Artificial Insemination by Donor. Beryl gazed before her, the flawless classical profile betrayed neither thought nor emotion. Monday was my day off from the restaurant, and the bedsit wasn't the place for relaxation and ease, more like paranoia, so I was glad to accept. I asked for my ticket in Godfrey's name at the table which served as Box Office, and the promised colleague overheard and introduced himself.

This was Willard, and he was gloomy. He'd been looking at the programme, and found that there were only three characters, and one set, so it was a cheap show. 'If that waffling fart Godfrey has this piece in mind for Belfast,' he said, 'he'll get us all assassinated.' Glancing at the two pages of blurred roneo which passed for a programme, I couldn't help being infected by my new colleague's gloom. The author's lonely and lifelong campaign for Artificial Insemination, the leading actor's many credits in avant-garde theatre, the other actors' total absence of credits of any kind, maybe Belfast wasn't going to be all that fine after all.

As it turned out, the show had its moments. The leading actor's part called for an elderly aristocrat, and he'd coated his thick mane with shoe-whitening, which dried under the lights. Every time the venerable lord shook his head, it was surrounded briefly by a shower of desiccated whitening falling gently to his shoulders. He looked, by the middle of Act One, to be suffering from extremely advanced dandruff. 'That'll be my part, if Godfrey's daft enough to do it,' muttered Willard. Since Willard was shining and comprehensively bald as Uncle Fester, this seemed reasonable casting to me, though I could see that without the personalized blizzard, there wasn't a lot of fun in the part.

The young milady, on the other hand, had a charming serenity, which, although it was at odds with the knotted moral problems posed in the story, was also quite a relief from them. 'I wonder if she's coming to Belfast with us?'

Willard was muttering, 'that could be why Godfrey's taking an interest. I'm quite interested myself, matter of fact. We could nip round afterwards eh? Make ourselves known to her.'

We'd reached the part in the play when the young lord has been found to be sterile, and the young wife discusses with her father-in-law how she is to bear the next in line for the title and the estates. The back wall of the set was entirely taken up with a large genealogical chart, and it was against this background that the young wife made a certain suggestion to the old man. When it had sunk in . . he was good on pauses . . he leapt back with extravagant senile vigour, arms akimbo, powdered whitening suspended in air about him. The line was something like 'Lucy, you surprise me', and it surprised everybody. He looked like Bertrand Russell in the snow. Curtain.

It may have been that Willard's boisterous enthusiasm and vigorous applause for the act ending had attracted some passing trade. Certainly the audience had grown by the end of the interval by two or three. The curtain rose. The ancient aristocrat, alone, crouched by the genealogical chart, his back to the audience. They were not to know, but during the interval, the new scion had been conceived and born, and his grandfather/father was adding his name to the family tree. He rose, turned to the audience, his face irradiated by a wondering pride. 'Good heavens,' he said, 'twenty-two inches.' Willard banged his fist and his head on the back of the seat in front of him, 'I'll play it, I'll play it,' he gasped.

The next day, Beryl phoned me to say she'd arranged for me to audition for a filmed commercial. She didn't seem interested in my report on the previous night's show. 'Artificial insemination by donor?' she said, 'in Belfast? Look, if I know anything about Godfrey, which isn't a lot, except he's got his hands on his mother's money, the only place that show is going is in the press release, so that we get the full attention of the Orange Lodge and the Bishop of All Ireland. It'd be the first time the country's been united since 1921. Now listen, it's a suit and tie job, they only want one, and he's got to be in his twenties.'

I arrived at the appointed time in the foyer of a Mayfair hotel, where the film company had booked a private room. People moved about with leisurely well-heeled grace, seemingly oblivious of the dreamy décor, insulated by wealth and luxury. This was the world of film, money wall to wall. I wondered if I should really be at the tradesmen's entrance, at least I'd know what to do there. A woman with a clipboard was scanning the room. I hurried over. I gave my name, and she ticked me off on her list, which seemed quite a long one. 'Please take a seat with the others,' she said, 'there's coffee if you wish it, just ask a waiter. We're doing you in batches of ten. I shall be calling your name in due course.' And she went about her business, ticking off names. I looked about the room. The rich international travellers, used to skilled and respectful attention all their waking hours, dissolved like a film before my eyes, and turned into a dole queue.

After forty minutes, the room had thinned out a bit, although others were still arriving, and my name was called out, along with nine others. The batch filed into a long narrow conference room, and stood before the table. Facing us sat three men in superb suits, and the lady with the clipboard. They didn't seem at all aware of the humiliation they were putting on the actors. Nor, for that matter, did the actors, they treated it all with an easy familiarity, including the Casting Director's alarming squint, which meant that when he pointed at one of them, he seemed to be looking at the next one along.

Each actor was asked his name, his age, his experience in film, and his height. As the questions got nearer, I was astonished to hear long accounts of extensive and wide experience in films I'd never heard of, and that each of them, from seeming-midgets to giants, gave his height as six foot. The finger pointed at me, I thought, and the eye was on the next one along. Rather than be missed out in the weird circus of embarrassment, I gabbled that I had no experience whatsoever of film and was five foot eight. Every head in the room clicked round to look at this eccentric dwarf, and the Casting Director stopped, finger pointed at me, his eye on the towering colossus next to me.

As we filed out, my neighbour in the line-up murmured, 'That was clever, got their attention all right that did. I must try it some time. I once turned up for *Peter Pan* auditions wearing a black eyepatch.'

'Did it do you any good?' I asked. 'Not really, I'd got the day wrong and they were auditioning for mermaids.'

The morning had been like looking at somebody else's holiday snapshots, a baffling, disorientating experience which I couldn't in any way relate to my craft, the pictures I'd seen, or, for that matter to anything I'd ever come across in my life. If it's possible to be mind-numbingly boring, insane, and criminally insulting all at the same time, that was what it had been. I told Gualterio about it that evening at work. 'We could have cast *Ben*

Hur. What nerd gives them enough money to do it? And where do they live when they're at home? under stones?'

'Is same with pantomime,' said Gualterio, sympathizing ruefully.

'You're an actor?'

'Dancer. I go for chorus in pantomime last year. The choreograph he say "Sorry, you too short." This year I go, same show, same choreograph. He say "Sorry, you too tall." I tell him, you no want dancer, you want piece elastic.'

Beryl turned out to be right about the insemination play. The advance press release had stirred up a classy storm, and the management had bowed graciously to public opinion. *Smiling Through* was to be the show in the serious spot instead. She told me the plot, a sad sentimental story of a courtship and a wedding brought to naught when a jealous rejected suitor shoots at the groom, the bride interposes herself and is killed in his place. The groom then spends the rest of his life in chaste mourning, to be united only in death. 'You're the faithful friend,' she said, 'Willard's the jealous rival, and you saw the bride at that damn fool club show.'

The mention of the young lady in want of insemination cheered me a great deal. Maybe Belfast would be very fine after all. 'It may not sound a ball of fire,' Beryl was saying, 'but it was a hit in its day.'

My mind was elsewhere. 'What was a hit in its day?' I said.

'*Smiling Through*.'

'When was its day?'

'Twenties, I think, but it's not costume,' she added hastily, 'we're not hiring anything.'

'Who's playing the bereaved groom?'

Beryl blushed, a faint, pink, blush, and changed the subject. 'You didn't get the commercial.' Sixth absolute of theatre: the truth is a tissue made of many lies.

The Lady of Notting Hill, I soon discovered, was Irish, and Godfrey had saved himself a rail and ferry fare by booking her from her Belfast home. The man was not quite so remote from reality as he looked at first sight, but then he couldn't be, not and still remember to get up in the morning. Pegeen, as she was called, had a kind of country radiance without her stage makeup, a freshness that made me wonder if my eyes were focusing properly. Glossy dark curls, grey eyes with enormous pupils, and a long-striding grace. I never really discovered whether she could act or not, but her bewildering beauty made her quite outstanding at borrowing props and furniture for the shows.

Carruthers, the designer, was a very large man with a ginger beard which seemed to have no discernible perimeter. It tufted relentlessly out of his shirt front, or any other small gap in his clothes. He smoked small brown wrinkly roll-ups, and talked, eloquently and incessantly. The shows got designed and dressed, but it was a mystery how it came about, because he and Pegeen always seemed to be in the Kitchen Bar next to the Empire, or walking about the city streets, talking. From time to time they would discover a second-hand furniture shop they hadn't previously betrayed, look in the window selecting the articles they would borrow for the next show, and then go in.

They explained their requirements rapidly to the shopkeeper, and before the man had had time to think,

Carruthers would raise the subject of Ireland's chances in the Four Nations, or maybe discourse on the Georgian poets, or Transubstantiation, while the shopkeeper struggled to keep his mind off Pegeen and hold on to his business's best interests. When fully launched into his chosen subject, Carruthers would gradually stretch his six-and-a-half feet of bulk and orange bristles along the shop counter, still talking, still clutching his damp squiggle of tobacco and brown paper. Between them, they could have borrowed Belfast City Hall clock.

Management had given a party so that the company could get to know one another, held in a small, ugly redbrick and pebbledash house on a road which runs alongside Belfast Lough. It wasn't made clear whose house it was, but Beryl and Francis, the Director and leading man, seemed comfortably at home in it. So did Godfrey. Every so often, I heard Beryl refer to Francis as 'Arthur'. I could imagine a scenario that would account for the mist of evasions and half-revealed titbits of information. The missing factor was Godfrey's mother. Was this perhaps the family home, out of which the mother had been affectionately eased, so that her beloved pixilated son could further his ambitions? Did she sit, day after day, grey and withdrawn, in a one-room turf cabin on the coast of far Donegal? Was Francis really someone else altogether? In Ireland, everything seemed both comic and tragic at the same time.

Francis was telling the company amusing and instructive anecdotes. Ewan MacMaster, he was saying, one of Ireland's great actor-managers, had made his name and fortune as a golden young man in *Smiling Through* in the West End. The wife he married at the height of his mainland fame as a front for his real sexual predilections, had hauled him back from the fleshpots and temptations of London, to tour Ireland in his own productions of all the major Shakespeare plays. A professor of literature in Dublin had once asked him whether he thought Hamlet had slept with Ophelia? 'In my company,' the great man replied gravely, 'invariably.' I swallowed a yawn and looked round the company. Pegeen was missing.

For some reason I couldn't explain to myself, I stepped out into the tiny entangled front garden. In the duck-egg blue of early summer morning, holding up the skirt of her pale linen dress in one hand, Pegeen, was walking steadily into the Lough. By the time I'd stripped off my socks, shoes and trousers so that I could wade out to her side, she was up to mid-thigh. 'Are you all right?' She stopped, turned her head briefly to see who it was. 'Ach hallo,' she said, her mind already turning to a far place, 'I was bored. When we have a party, we have songs, music for dancing, a ceilidh.' She listened to ancient music, and was her own ceilidh.

We grew chilled, but neither of us wanted to break the moment. Finally, 'Come,' she said, and we took a bus to the Docks, where we found bacon sandwiches, and then another bus out again through the city, to Cove Hill, which we climbed, finding tiny wild strawberries among the rocks by the path. Because the surrounding land is flat, and laid out in small fields, it felt like a mountain. Making love in a tangle of clothes on the peak, the Queen of Tara in her scullion's arms, in a land of mysterious stories, we suddenly remembered the rehearsal, and hurtled down to be in time, giggling and whooping as the steep path accelerated the descent, helpless and hysterical.

That night, I slept the sleep of a stone crusader on a slab, there was barely a ruckle in the sheets where I'd been. Belfast was going to be very fine indeed.

I shared a room in Miss Black's digs with George, who had left the Navy to try a mid-career switch to stage management. Miss Black was intrigued by the undisturbed sheets, but clearly couldn't find her way round to querying it directly.

'Were you very late getting in last night?' she said, 'I didn't hear you come in at all.'

George had the neat good looks, rosy cheeks, laughter lines at the corners of mouth and eyes, that bespeak an anguished inner turmoil. He was occasionally the victim of appalling nightmares, in which he dreamt he was swallowing a snake. He would levitate, rigid and galvanic from his bed, hit the floor running, still deep asleep, hurtle to the bathroom, turn the cold tap on full, and wash the snake from his mouth, and return to his bed. I had to turn the gushing tap off more than once.

In her ongoing search to get some inkling of the nature of the strange men under her roof, Miss Black unwittingly fed George's night terrors by telling a story of a previous lodger. 'Few weeks ago,' she told them one breakfast time, 'I had a most respectable and quiet young lady come from Chipperfield's Circus. She had two suitcases, big ones, but she wouldn't let me help her upstairs with them, not her, very adamant about it. When she'd settled in, and came down for a cup of tea, she says don't you bother with cleaning the room, or anything like that, I'll see to that. Only me snake's in there. It wouldn't do you any harm, she says, but if it escapes, that's me act gone. Couple a days went by, and she was as tranquil and decent a young woman as ever lodged here, borrowing me broom and dustpan and that to tidy the room. Then one time I was passing the door to her room, and saw it was open a crack, and the young lady out, I knew for sure. Oh my God, I thought, I'd better close that. But you know it was very hard not to just have a peek in for a glance of the python. The tip of me cat's tail was just disappearing down its heathen gob.'

She looked from George's appalled face to mine, but neither of us could formulate a suitable response. We'd come to an arrangement already that when one of us wanted to entertain a guest, he would leave the light on, so the other one would know to stay out for an hour or so. This wasn't tedious, because the pub round the corner served all hours of the day or night. If it was after legal hours, you tapped with a half-crown piece on the green-tiled wall by the back door, which would be opened by the barman on a smoke-filled interior crammed with roaring dockers. How he heard the tapping of a coin in all that row was an impenetrable mystery. 'Come you in quickly,' he said, 'and for God's sake don't make a sound, or you'll have the Polis down on us all.' Looking at George after the story of the python, I suspected I might be tapping on the wall quite soon.

The Director, in an ideal world, would not have been cast as John, the male lead in *Smiling Through*. It's set around 1924 or so . . . there's still flower-decked hedges, with handsome young squires, and the thwarted lover is a subaltern, with the fatal revolver in his Sam Browne.

With his sleek dyed hair and precise, clipped theatrical diction, Francis seemed essentially a man of the forties or fifties. You could easily imagine him, on the bridge of a doomed destroyer, gazing stoically into the bucketsful of water hurled at him to represent Atlantic spray for studio purposes.

Striding down a country lane, even one lovingly painted for him on the stage floor by Carruthers, Francis wasn't really at home. He looked as if he was only out for the day and couldn't wait to get back to the smoke and the clubs. 'If my family could see me now,' he muttered to himself as he straightened his hunting cravat. Most of the cast had to age, some forty years, during the course of the play, and perhaps Francis came into his own by the time he came to his peaceful death in the dying sunlight of his flower-filled garden, but then again, he still looked as if he was waiting for cocktails. Unfortunately, his youthful ghost appears for the final meeting with his long-dead beloved, so it was a very quick change, and back to square one.

Moonyeen, played by Pegeen, didn't have to age of course, she got herself shot in all her youthful glory. Nor did Willard, the jealous rival, he dies in some heroic and remorse-filled way. All he had to do was wait for curtain-call. And there he was, his Sam Browne and bald pate gleaming in the backstage light, right by the onstage dressing-room that had been rigged up out of hessian by Carruthers for Pegeen's quick-change into Moonyeen's bridal gown. Willard had never quite figured out how, since he was the one who so suavely introduced himself to her after the Artificial Insemination show, she'd become so mysteriously preoccupied since their arrival in Belfast. But he wouldn't let her down, oh no, no matter what emergency she might have with snap-fastener or zip, he was on hand to help, sturdy and true.

I'd become aware that there was something transcendent about this particular night when I was accosted by a small boy in a ragged pullover, shorts down to his calves, and laceless shoes, right by the Stage Door. The lad had a sort of crude dummy made out of an old shirt, with cardboard face and hands. For a moment I thought it was an outstandingly early Guy Fawkes (in July), but then I saw that the dummy's name was written neatly on a large label on its chest. 'This is Bradley,' said the boy. I shook hands with the mannikin and said how d'you do. I had a holdall under my arms, the leather handles dangling down. The dummy craned over sideways to examine the nearest handle. 'Bradley thinks it's a lobster,' said the boy. We could have been at Odin's table, caught by the mischievous tricks of Loki, the troublemaker. Ireland, land of mystery, myth and legend. 'Bradley wants a shilling for the gas,' said the boy.

So. *Smiling Through.* Last scene. It is evening. The bright viridian raffia grass and the wax flowers glow in the setting sun. Dear old doddering Best Friend arrives. A game of dominoes is proposed, so that John may for a short while forget to brood on his enduring loss. I creep geriatrically to the garden table, while John goes off to get the pieces. Swifter than thought, he reappears, with the dominoes. Be it noted that from his re-entrance on, the audience doesn't see the tragic hero's face. This is because it's no longer the Director, it's George, as his double, identically dressed, silent as a monument . . his other nightmare is being asked to talk and act at the same time.

The reason for this slow-motion taradiddle is that the star is even now quick-changing in the wings right by us. When we think he's made it, George will die peacefully in his stead, dear old doddering Best Friend will depart, thinking his old friend has fallen asleep, and John's youthful spirit will appear, ethereal, but otherwise still sturdily loyal in his love. He will gaze up into the moonlight, stage left, which is even now beginning to overtake the late mellow glow of the setting sun. *Then* Moonyeen, lovely and true as she was all those years ago, will glide swanlike down the moonbeams into his arms. Not a dry eye in the house.

'Look at you, falling asleep over your dominoes again,' I burbled, 'I've told you before, you should choose a less exciting game this close to your bedtime, it overtires you . .'

'What in God's name's the clown garbling on about now?' hissed Francis from the wings, 'Act Five? Get him off, *now*, they'll all have gone home by the time I get on.'

'I shall have to tell your housekeeper you've nodded off,' I chuntered as I went, 'it's no use me trying to . . .'

'God dammit!' from the wings.

A magical, blessed silence falls on the house. John enters, ghostly, and stands, silvered by the moonlight. And he stands. And he stands. No Moonyeen. 'Moonyeeen,' calls John, in tones of yearning edged by desperation. I dashed to her hessian tent.

Willard bars the way, 'She's got a quick-change,' he hisses. I sidestepped him, pulled aside the hessian. 'She's off,' I said. 'She's waiting for a safety-pin.'

Sitting there with the patience of a porcelain martyr, she'd soften the heart of Genghis Khan.

'Bloody get on that stage!'

'Mooonyeeen . . .' the cry again from the stage, a coyote on heat. The dead hero examines the flowers of the garden, pistil by pistil. Willard saves the night: in the least secure falsetto since Mickey Rooney's Puck, he calls to the stage . . . 'I'm coming John,' he cries.

And finally she glided on. Her charming disarray, the sugar-white dress falling away from her rosy shoulders, the gauze of the torn bodice gripped in apprehension of further collapse, brought the audience to their feet. There may have been further dialogue, but there was no following that *coup de théâtre.* The Director waved his hand up and down behind his dishevelled bride's back, as an indication to the Prompt Corner to get the rag down, and quick. The audience was ecstatic. The curtain came down at last, rose again on the tableau, came down, rose again on the assembled beaming cast, and still they roared their approval. Whatever their interpretation of the spectacle that night, they knew in their bones that it was unique.

That night, I discovered I wasn't the only one who was peering into Celtic mystery. Beryl was in Francis's dressing-room, Godfrey was to treat them to a candle-lit dinner. He was learning to be an impresario the hard way, but his mother's money seemed to be holding up under the strain. As I passed, Beryl called out to me, her eyes bright as a girl's, 'We all know that you two are doing it, and we've been wondering where, but do try to keep your hands off her during the show.'

George, of course, thought it was all his fault, though

nobody blamed him. He could hardly have done anything about the safety-pin while he was onstage, stiff dead, but he was sorely in need of consolation, and made sure I had a half-crown piece for the pub wall. He was starting to be anxious about Miss Black as well. She might not be too pleased if she found out she was giving free lodging to an extra guest.

When he got his new friend to the digs, he explained this anxiety to him, and proposed that he should piggyback him in and up the stairs. That way Miss Black would only hear one set of footsteps. The friend thought it had a certain romance, and agreed. As they crabbed along the hallway, the tinkle of the radio came from the kitchen. Never mind, perhaps that would deaden the noise of George's return from work, having put on ten stone and an extra four limbs. They reached the stairs, and began the laborious ascent, as the kitchen door clicked quietly open. There was a moment as she took in the scene, then 'Ooom, cripples now is it?' And the door closed again.

7

Monkey business

The downstairs windows of the bus were impenetrably mottled with a black and dark yellow filth, so I got up to take a look out from the open platform at the back. Behind, and receding fast, was a sign painted in large white letters on the iron bridge across the road, 'Welcome to Oldham,' it said, 'Home of the Tubular Bandage'. I grabbed my old leather suitcase and scuttered back to the platform. Even in my panicky haste, I noticed the lower deck was now populated by pale misshapes of the industrial ballrace. The bus had passed through Oldham, and was now taking the workers home to their council estates. 'I wanted the Town Centre,' I told the conductor. 'Well, all right, you have it then,' said the man, 'nobody else wants it.' Then he pulled out a rubber monkey-mask from his tunic pocket, put it on, and crouched, swinging his bony arms down by his knees, wrists well below the cuffs. 'This is an express bus,' he chittered.

'Could you put me down at the next stop please?'

'I'm sure he'll do his best, but his brakes have been playing him up. Would it be all right if he changed down to walking pace? Mind, that might bring another problem, he's been sweating over his double-de-clutching, very impatient man, my mate. I'll see what he says.'

'I'm going to the Coliseum,' I told him, in a whimper of anxiety.

Immediately, the lower deck broke out into loud private and public argument about where exactly the Coliseum was, and whether I'd be able to use my ticket from Manchester to retrace my route. The bus slowed down, and I hurled myself off amid a pandemonium of good-hearted advice, and flapped a hand towards the departing chimpanzee, now hanging from the back rail of the platform, and waving down oncoming traffic so that I could cross the road to catch the next bus back into town.

Drivers in the traffic jam thus created beamed their appreciation and pipped their horns joyfully in appreciation of the ad hoc street theatre. 'He's always doing it,' said the young woman waiting with me at the bus stop, rubbing one bare mottled leg against the other in the scouring November wind, 'he'll get his self done one o' these days, he's supposed to wear his cap when he's on duty.'

'I wanted the Coliseum,' I told her.

'You have to be a member,' she said, 'but my mate's a cleaner there, and she gets us tickets. The bar's very nice, you meet all sorts of different people, not just mucky sods. It's in Fairbottom Street.'

'I'm joining the company,' I said.

Her pale eyes focused on me swiftly, and with keen interest. 'Nice,' she said, 'there's not a lot of work about. I used to be a model, but they don't want you when you've got stretch marks.'

R
E
J
E
C
T
S

D
I
R
E
C
T

it said down the window at the corner of Fairbottom Street.

Joining an acting company can be like becoming part of a small enclosed cosmos. Even a two-day radio engagement, or a one-day extra part on a film, encloses the artiste in a recognizable pattern, where each member knows and keeps to their own orbit, linked to the surrounding universe. Oldham Rep was not like that. The turbulent community that swirled outside the Stage Door was too powerfully honest, too dramatically and drably colourful, it overwhelmed artifice. In self-defence, much of the company closed themselves off. It was only after Roland, the leading character actor had moved gratefully out of the dressing-room we shared, that it dawned on me that the man simply didn't like me. The pink drum of gents' urinal air-freshener which appeared on the wall between the two mirrors had been Roland's genteelly brutal way of indicating that he didn't enjoy the stench of my pipe.

Roland's private and unexpressed rage against my proletarian crudeness was exacerbated, rather than mitigated, by my sweaty enthusiasm for the very actresses Roland had lately queened it over. The used condoms wrapped in lavatory paper and dropped in the dressing-room waste-bin were a grief. The clumsy bull-headed habits of my apprenticeship in Leicester, and latterly in Belfast, grated sorely on Roland's fastidious, perfumed, well-tailored sensibility. The reek of my sexual encounters in the town was doubly infuriating to Roland, who washed before, after and even during his furtive homosexual encounters. I didn't mind getting dirty, Roland loathed it. Each of us was mad in his own way, but I got more fun.

The climax was to come in the Shakespeare, a strikingly picturesque Victorian gin palace of a pub behind the theatre. The landlord, Richard, was a stage hypnotist, prestidigitator and Punch and Judy man. His wife had been a shapely showgirl, but she declined into a kind of inert, expressionless quietude after marriage. Her husband's dashing courtship, she'd soon discovered, had been dedicated to recruiting a free conjuror's assistant for his occasional dates at Masonic dinners and crumbling nightspots. She would very occasionally serve behind the bar, looking like a dead-eyed barmaid at the Folies Bergères, as painted by Renoir. The only time she showed any animation was when the huge Alsatian guard-dog shoved his massive head up her skirt.

Eventually, she was to leave her husband for a Chinese contortionist and juggler, whose one-week stand at

Huddersfield was marred on the Monday evening. The betrayed husband turned up in the royal box, in the company of a flat-footed homicidal ex-Military Policeman. Richard's eyes burned with hypnotic power over a ferocious Vandyke moustache and tuft as he tapped the ash off an enormous Cuban cigar onto the stage before the hapless performer. 'The juggling left something to be desired,' reported the *Huddersfield Examiner*, 'but the contortions of this talented performer were greeted with deserved enthusiasm.'

We'd just finished a fortnight's run of a new play, which was set in a Dublin suburb. The central character had been a member of an IRA cell, and now wants out. His area commander, which was me, calls at the house to tell him he can't quit, he knows too much. The hero insists that he wants to devote the rest of his life to importing plastic Christmas trees from Japan. The confrontation between the two is quiet, still; the only movement over a long fifteen minutes or more is when the commander moves briefly to the window over the street and back, and then tells his reluctant soldier that there's man down there outside with orders to kill, should the interview go the wrong way. If the commander shows himself at the window, the man will go away.

That Saturday, the enormity of the forces at work in the scene swept over me, and I lost my temper for real. Bill, who played the soldier, was my friend, and now shared the dressing-room, a gentle, easygoing, quietly humorous young man. Rage boiled up in me; the neat suburban room spun round my head in a blur of blood. I couldn't unjam my jaws to carry on with the dialogue, and turned my back on the audience to regain control, a struggle which seemed to go on for hours, with absolutely nothing happening, until my sanity returned, and I was able to finish the scene. I apologized ruefully to Bill afterwards, privately thanking God that the prompter was away from the corner, confident that everyone was secure on their lines by now, and so didn't feed me a cue I wouldn't have been able to articulate. 'What're you sorry about?' said Bill, 'it's a long time since I knew an audience so held by a pause that long.' This puzzled me mightily: if losing control altogether would involve an audience so, what was all the other stuff for?

Roland, who had a fortnight out during this run, was just back from a break at home with his mum. He sat on a stool at the corner of the long bar in the Shakespeare, his brown velour trilby on the stool next, brim up to preserve the stylish snap, the pale leather hatband as pristine as when it left the shop. I greeted him, and in my preoccupation with my insight into my trade failed to notice the disdainful nod my colleague gave me. 'Caught the show tonight,' said Roland to the ornate mirror behind the bar. 'Curious that there are those among us who can't come to terms with their dialogue even after a month,' he said, and then went back to his conversation with the glowingly handsome young man standing at his side.

The Saturday night tide of noise was rising. Richard was doing a trick behind the bar, in which he was furiously smoking a cigarette, exclaiming the while that he really must give up the filthy habit. Then he threw the half-smoked cig in the washing-up water, and lo, he had a cigarette in his hand, lit, and exactly the length of the one floating in the soapy water. He continued to complain about the difficulty of giving up smoking, and throw successive lit cigarettes away, until four sodden half-smoked rejects lay in the sink, and Richard was contentedly smoking a briar pipe. Enthusiastic applause from the customers.

'Hey,' I said, 'that's my pipe!' 'Is it? I was wondering whose it was.' Much impressed, I took it back and examined it. It was indeed my pipe. How in the world had Richard slanced it from the ashtray, where I'd placed it so as not to offend Roland, in full view of the customers, *and* kept it burning while he manoeuvred the four cigarettes? It would normally have gone out within seconds. As I turned it over to make sure it really was my own pipe, the burning tobacco and ash showered out into Roland's velour trilby on the stool at his side. I snatched up the hat, reached over the bar, and dunked it hastily in the sink.

Roland seemed not to have noticed this panicky rescue, but the other customers roared again as I picked off shreds of moist tobacco and paper, shook off as much water as I could, and returned the hat to the stool, brim up as before. Roland remained deep in his intimate conversation. He'd trained himself to close his ears to the vulgar rowdyism of Oldham pubs, which tended to sound as if there was a full-scale riot going on inside, especially on a Saturday night. If I couldn't see that Oldham Rep was a step up between vagabond and the West End, Roland could.

His new friend saw the hat kerfuffle all right. From his vantage point round the corner of the bar, he would see the sink fully, but they weren't yet closely acquainted, and for all the young man knew, this might be some kind of Saturday night ritual in the Shakespeare, to which Roland was a willing party. Certainly no harm had been done. With reasonable luck, I hoped, the hat would at least be dry by the time Roland came to put it on and leave. An Indian meal was proposed. Roland rose, picked up the hat. I closed my eyes. Roland adjusted his fine overcoat, which fitted snugly round his portly hips, and made for the door, followed by his friend.

There were few in this company that Roland thought worthy of his farewells. Most tended to ribaldry, like a quick chorus of 'Our lodger's such a nice young man . . .', and they proved his point again when he turned at the door, raising a hand into the lowering tobacco smoke. 'Good night Richard,' he boomed into the momentarily quietened room, 'and thank you for your hospitality.' Richard, who had seen everything since the Pharaohs, paused as he pumped a pint, took a good look, his luxuriant eyebrows working like pepper-and-salt caterpillars on his brow, and then nodded goodnight.

Squeezed by Roland's sleek head, the hatband had released a trickle of tobacco-stained water, which coursed down his forehead, settled for a moment on the bridge of his Napoleonic nose, then set off again for his chin. The customers thought the whole scene excellent, and clapped their hands with enthusiasm, with hoarse shouts of 'More!' and 'Gerrum off!' Roland's nostrils flared briefly, he waved a patrician hand at the rabble, then led his new friend into the night, dabbing with an immaculate lawn handkerchief at what he guessed to be unwelcome perspiration scalding the corner of his eye.

Besides the instant and intimate biographies at every encounter, and the mild artistic elevation of fortnightly rep, there were other benefits for a young actor in Oldham. A vigorous Manchester and Leeds radio drama, and the booming Granada TV output, all within easy access. I applied to all of them, writing and phoning directors, in hopes of raising my £15 a week salary to something from which I could set a bit aside for leaner times. It seemed there was nothing that couldn't be had in this town for the price of a pint, and I found a couple of rabbiting dogs I could borrow, then rescued my father's gun from among the fluff at my mother's house.

Smuggling the gun, for which I didn't have a certificate, into my bedsit, wasn't easy, but the dog man ran me up a couple of stout canvas pouches, linked by a yoke, and I could carry the gun, broken into its separate pieces, round my neck under a short coat. It was a mite awkward on the bus, or clanking upstairs to my room, but if anyone noticed, they probably thought I was just another Oldham crazy, coming home with some non-ferrous I'd pinched for private trading. On a good weekday, when I wasn't called for rehearsal, I could get out onto the hillsides, and knock over a couple of rabbits, out of which I rewarded the dog man, and got myself a free supper or two.

I found the borrowed dogs were impossible to control. Crossbred, rough-coated whippet/collies, they were around twenty-four inches at the shoulder. They seemed to regard collars and leads as dangerous or insulting, shying and ducking away if I tried to put them on them. But I rarely had to pay for them on the bus, they sloped silently up to the top deck, and lay curled under the seat until I rose to get off. If the conductor spotted them, I often found myself involved in a long account of dogs the man had loved and lost. One in particular, an East European who brought a touch of the endless icebound plains to Oldham Transport, spoke of Ilych, his Great Dane, who would respond to commands in Russian, English and Ukrainian.

'Woss like human that dog,' he said, wiping away a huge tear with a hand like a spade, 'mose intelligent animal I ever knew.' 'What happened to it?' I asked. 'Woss shot, chasing sheeps,' said the conductor, and lumbered off down the bus giving an impression of the Wehrmacht's Retreat from Moscow.

The dogs, it turned out, knew their jobs and mine far better than ever I would, and were also considered legitimate targets by every sheep farmer on the Pennines. However, whenever a farmer appeared, the dogs were nowhere to be seen. There was the golf course, where the greensman was pathetically grateful for my patrol, provided I was away by eight a.m., when the first golfers might be tee-ing off. One way and another, life was looking good. Then came the biggie: two episodes of a serial for Granada. It fitted with two weeks out at Oldham, and the money, seventy pounds an episode, made me dizzy.

The soap had been running for nine years, and a cold draught was beginning to make itself felt round the ratings. Heads would have to roll. The new Producer, a Valium addict who had twitches where no one else could achieve them without studying yoga, told me everything was under wraps, but a favourite character was to die of a spectacular heart-attack. She didn't know yet, but the new boss had watched twenty-six episodes, and decided to weed out those characters which bored him. This nationally loved character would be the sacrifice to bring a blessing on the ratings.

I was to be the hitherto unseen son-in-law, but the filming of the funeral, and my two and a half scenes, would be recorded at the end of the week in which the nation's elderly sweetheart would demonstrate her dying skills to a grief-stricken public. The whole thing was Top 'A' Classified Most Secret, said the Producer, swallowing two more pills, and winking uncontrollably. When we gathered for the read-through, there was an atmosphere of embattled gloom. Bill, my friend from Oldham, was by now a permanent player in the soap, so I sat next to him, it seemed safer. The friend and boozing companion of the doomed actress was the organist in the serial's Chapel. She sat, looking like an empurpled Churchill during Britain's Darkest Days, clutching her script in an iron and vengeful grip.

An array of writers and executives were in attendance, all with yellow briefcases held defensively upright on their laps. The Director of the week, an innocent young lamb thrown into the slaughter-pen far too early because more experienced directors had better footwork, had trouble with a dry throat as he asked the Studio Manager to read the stage directions into the dialogue, so that they could check for timing. 'There's just one thing,' said the condemned woman's colleague, turning an even darker purple.

'I'd like to get on, Violet,' said Michael.

'There's just one thing,' she insisted with Dreadnought determination, 'and I want it noted.'

'Very well,' he said, ' 'erm, thank you, stop the clock.'

'I will *not* play the organ, there's nothing in the contract.'

Yellow briefcases snapped open, pens were fumbled out. To everyone's relief, the touching sight of Violet playing the pedal organ for her friend's premature death at sixty-eight, was barely a thirty-second excision. The rest of the cast were hardly mollified.

'In the midst of death in a soap,' murmured Bill, 'your own kidney-shaped swimming-pool is at serious risk.' Two veteran actors sitting behind us tittered down their noses like choirboys.

In one of the bizarreries I was beginning to get used to in my own life, which backtracked and lurched forward, driven by impulses I rarely understood until long after, filming of the burial was to take place before the death, and my scene of the tussle over who was to pay for it was rehearsed two days later, to be recorded just before the funeral baked meats in the Chapel Vestry.

Arthur, one of the veterans, detested the acclaim that his new career in TV had brought him. Members of the public would accost him with loud and egregious overfamiliarity, 'Aren't you somebody famous?' He referred to them as 'the neck-less.' The company cruised through the mean streets of North-East Manchester in black limousines, on our way to the unrevealed destination, every face a twice-weekly visitor in seven and a half million households.

When we reached the cemetery, which was surrounded by high-rise council flats, there was a dense crowd of happy fans, held back by ropes, and smiling policemen. Every balcony was crammed with cheerfully waving enthusiasts. Scraps of paper were thrust out for autographing by the mourners, 'Could you say "Best love to Rosie please?" You're my mum's greatest fan.' Arthur, his eyes baleful half-moons of malice, scribbled W.C. Fields, Gracie, or Henry Irving Bart, indiscriminately. 'One of these days, Henry,' he said, 'I shall be assassinated by some enraged member of the Great Unwashed.'

Fortunately, the shots were mute, except for Arthur's peroration and prayers, which would be dubbed in later. This was as well, because the holiday shouts of the milling public drowned out even the bullhorn instructions of the Unit Manager, Paddy. Some eager designer had suggested that the camera should be set looking up out of the grave. The late lamented's view of her own funeral.

'Where are the crippled dwarfs and terminally diseased fallen women, Paddy?' Arthur enquired, 'this is a Bergman film we're doing here I take it?'

Arthur was a small, square, balding man, with a clipped ginger Army moustache, whose experience as a Hussar had left him with a permanent fascination with any mode of transport that was faster than a horse. I worshipped him on sight, but my idol was cut out of my little scene, partly because I was making such a meal of it, knowing that I had an extra thirty seconds to play with, but also because Arthur's middle-aged frivolity in the midst of the serial's crisis grated on an already sorely pressed Director. Also, as the graveside mourners rehearsed the return along the studio street, Arthur's gold-rimmed spectacles were to be seen gleaming from the set's GPO letterbox, and a small hand waved small cheerful Pickwickian gestures to passing colleagues.

After that, I couldn't look Arthur in the face without sniggering uncontrollably.

Without Arthur, the scene was a three-hander. Stephanie ('Our Lily'), me ('Our Lily's Wilf'), and Royston, the Insurance Man. Michael moved his three actors about with mounting despair, hoping to get some reality out of what was in reality not much. The only thing that gave it any meat was that there wasn't enough in the old lady's insurance policy to bury her. Time clunked by, and still Michael shuffled his three cards, hoping that someone would Spot the Lady. Tears stood in Stephanie's Viking eyes, a vein pulsed in Royston's temple. Finally, I remembered my controlled explosion back at the Rep. 'How would it be,' I offered, 'if we all stood right where we are, and we play it Wilf wants to know if there's enough to bury his mother-in-law, and is in haste to prevent his wife from dissolving in tears of grief and guilt, Lily wants urgently to dissolve in tears and guilt, and the Insurance Man urgently wants to be anywhere but where he is?'

'We're a bit pushed,' said Michael, looking at his watch, and trying urgently to stop his movements from being jerky, 'but OK, let's try it that way, standing still.'

It wasn't *Macbeth*, but it worked at long last. It dawned on me that the Director wasn't always right, and that maybe I'd picked up a useful experience after all, not just an embarrassing one. Drama may well be spectacle, visible movement does represent inner impulses, but in its essence, it's empathetic magic. Seventh absolute: in the silences above, below, and in between the lines, lies the action.

The final scene in the Vestry was every bit as glum as

such scenes are supposed to be, but seldom are. The Series Producer hadn't begged me to accept an extended contract on much better terms, the writers weren't clamouring to develop Our Lily's Wilf into a national institution, the permanent citizens of the soap had been made harshly aware that they weren't as permanent as all that, and two out of the three cameras broke down. The cast and crew had been working with the briefest of breaks since nine that morning, and it was now six forty-five in the evening. His last scene finished, as he thought, Arthur had boarded his beloved Daimler Coupé, and sped off for the London train without waiting for a clear or even changing.

'I was just having a rinse in the train lavatory, prior to a sherry and a light supper, when I heard some garbled mention on the tannoi that might have been my name. I returned to my first-class compartment, and stuck my head out of the window. I was instantly singled out by two men in blue, and escorted back along the platform like a criminal. They even had the gall to ask me for my autograph in their notebooks.'

Makeup had long gone home, so it was a pale and shiny Arthur who took his place in the street outside the Chapel for yet another take. Inside, the remains of the lettuce was limp and darkening, a few slices of curling ham glistened oily in the studio lighting. I put my aching feet up on the table as we waited. 'Take your feet off my Vestry table,' said Violet. I thought at first she was making a weary joke, but no such thing. 'Get those feet off my table,' she repeated, her sparse eyebrows shooting up sideways to her cruel perm. After nine years, the part was playing her.

The studio relapsed into silence. I wondered if a stroll round the studio and away from the lights might ease my aching limbs. Cameramen sat on the pedestals of their cameras, or in other sets, cobwebs hung above and around the tops of the flats like Miss Haversham's Wedding Feast, and it crossed my idle mind that Dickens takes you no more into the mind of that batty old lady and her tormenting niece than I myself could read the pale blank faces in the half dark around me.

Arthur came up to me where I stood, in the open area where the cameras manoeuvred from setting to setting. 'All right then Henry, just a quick chorus, "Abide with Me", I'll take the cornet, you're on trombone.' He jiggled his imaginary keys to be sure the valves were free, cocked a solemn eye to see if my slide was mobile and ready to play, opened and blew through his imaginary spit-valve, with a grave moue of apology for the pool of imaginary spit at my feet, pressed his imaginary instrument to his lips, blew out his cheeks like Dizzie Gillespie, nodded, and we were off. Arthur's wavering, mournful, unwarmed-up cornet soared in B Flat among the cobwebs, my extended fart of the harmony labouring up after it. The rump of the cast sat still at their places round the Vestry table in the only real light, like a *Last Supper* painted by L.S. Lowry. There was a reverent silence as we finished, melancholy with long-cherished and now lost hope. Then the crew, who were on fat overtime, applauded warmly.

A hundred and forty pounds wages in one week, plus overtime at a pound a minute, was an event to be shared and celebrated. I hurried back to Oldham and the Klondyke saloon that the Shakespeare became on a

Friday night. I missed the express bus, so it was after closing-time by the time I got back. The pub was silent. A glimmer of light around the tightly curtained windows. Richard *never* closed on time. He made regular appearances at the Magistrates' Court, a bit like a court of Lilliputians passing judgement on Gulliver. I went round the back, and clambered over the gate, determined to share my elation, if only with Richard.

The bar was silent, the pumps shrouded with dishcloths as if they would never be used again. Roland, alone on his stool, his head in his hands. As I came in, he looked up, and finished his gin and tonic, stood, and started to walk towards me, his step firm. 'Ah,' he said. 'Where is everybody?' I asked. 'Games Room,' said Roland. 'Mine host has had a tip-off that there's to be a police raid. Quite right too, he extends hospitality to riff-raff; burglars, pimps and whores every one. Present company not excepted.' He was getting quite close to me. 'He's now giving a demonstration of crude puppetry to the assembled rubble of what was once a noble industrial town.'

I went out and across the corridor. I peeped into the Games Room, aware that Roland was close at my heels. Sure enough, there they sat, drunkards and wastrels, even the odd honest pauper, their bodies broken by byssinosis, coughs forgotten. Not a glass in sight, they gazed up, mouths agape on ragged teeth, as Punch's murderous plot unfolded. I closed the door, and turned back to Roland to thank him for this strange information. Roland's fist hit me in the middle of my face with enough force to crack my head back against the door I'd just closed. A chorus of 'Come in officer' and 'Shaddap you noisy bastards!' joined Punch's discordant shriek for a moment, and then fell silent again. 'That's the way to do it!' screamed Punch.

I dashed back in the bar in search of ice and something to mop up the squirting blood from my nose, holding my hand under my nose. Roland must have had the hat cleaned, he stood at the open door of the bar, the velour as jaunty and pristine as before, buttoning his overcoat for the exit line of the week as I dripped generously into the sink behind the bar. 'That's for the hat,' said Roland, haughty, 'among other things.' And he was gone. The back way. The police were coming in the front.

As Roland unbolted the back gate, a young constable posted outside assumed that this was a fellow officer letting him in. Roland was as rattled at the sudden encounter as was the constable, but the policeman recovered first, and arrested the actor on charges he feverishly imagined he'd be able to dream up later. Inside, a sergeant and another constable were watching a re-run of Punch and Judy, and I was still dripping in the sink. 'Nosebleed,' I told the young officer, who was biting his lip and wondering if he might not be better suited in Serious Crime.

Interlude

She rests her round bum
On the iron rail
Corroded by sea-frets
November Manhattan
Late night by the Battery
Looking out and across
The United Fruit Co. dock
Towards forgotten England
And the words process
Round and around
Her small round head
To tell her lover her news.
Out on the Hudson
A small bell clanks
A white light winks on
Winks off, bleak.
Three thousand miles back
Lover opens her letter
In a room where the Euston lines
Meet for a metal chat
A hand-cream smirch
Her left thumb left

Smells sweet and stale
On ivory paper, green ink
Quite pretty really
'I
just
don't
love
you
any
more'
It says
And one big sob
Bursts in his head
And goes out
Like a light on water.

8

Hits, misses, and high-speed myth

Towards the end of my Oldham contract, I made my first TV script sale, £200 in advance for a thirty-month option. I watched myself, intrigued, as I took the BBC envelope from the Stage Door letter rack, opened it, and took out the cheque. It looked marvellous. It looked *marvellous*. Half a year's income, and another two hundred to come when it was broadcast. Phew.

I'd learned by now that just as the actor's craft has no permanence, no yesterday or tomorrow, only now, and with this particular audience, so is the money as short-lived as a mayfly. I bought myself a Burberry overcoat, three drip-dry shirts, and a pair of jodhpur boots from Burton's. The fashion was for Chelsea boots, flimsy and elastic-sided, so I went one up-market. I also treated Bill and his wife to a rabbit supper with a great deal of expensive wine. And I bought all round at the Shakespeare. Roland toasted my future good fortune in a very large gin and tonic, though he didn't look at me while he was saying it. 'Boom,' I said in my head as I walked about, 'boom boom.'

Beryl got me a tour, first date the Lyceum Sheffield. I

got the digs list from the resident Stage Manager, who was working on the Sunday get-in with Andy, the Tour Manager, and Judith, ASM, known as One-amp. The payphone was by the Stage Door, and phoning wasn't easy as baskets of props, scenery and furniture were manhandled in with many a shout, bang, and curse. The first answer was a man who told me in a loud clear voice that I must have dialled a wrong number, because his name wasn't Minnie, he didn't live here, and nor did anybody else, he'd have to shift over to get a decent-sized cat in. He was in a hurry, he said, but he was just one of those people who can't resist picking up a phone if it's ringing. He'd have to be off now, tara, he said, and put the phone down.

I dialled again very carefully, checking the number on the list digit by digit. This time, after a surprisingly long wait, during which I was free to register that it had gone quiet around me, finally a woman answered. She seemed uncertain about her number, even indifferent: if this wasn't the number you dialled, she said, why had I dialled it? Her bus was due any minute, she said. It crossed my mind that I must be waking the household from deep Sunday afternoon snoozes, full of Yorkshire pudding and slabs of roast beef, so I enunciated my words, in as reassuring a way as I could manage with my tuppence running out. I must have sounded like a serial heavy-breather. Was I speaking to Minnie Gent, number three Mafeking Street? I fed another two pennies in: what were her terms for actors? The woman's voice rose in pitch, so that I had to hold the receiver away from my ear. She said she wasn't used to answering personal questions from complete strangers, this was certainly

Mafeking Street, if I must know, but she wasn't going to get Minnie to the phone, whoever she was. This was a public phone box, she said, and she was waiting for a bus. I told her I was looking for good pro digs. I'm a respectable married woman, she shouted, and rang off.

I finally got through to Rosie Meiklejohn, who had her own phone, though she seemed apprehensive about it, her voice quavering, and distant (she treated it like a cobra, holding it vertical away from her face). I stayed there often over the years, sunk in a goose-down mattress, with a huge fire of miner's concession coal thundering up the chimney, but that Sunday afternoon, if she'd been asking fourpence a night to sleep draped over a rope across the cellar, I'd've taken it. As I rang off, I saw Andy, One-amp and the Stage Manager beaming at me from the doorway. The Stage Manager apologized with an attempt at straight-faced sincerity; he'd forgotten to tell me that some landladies had their own telephone system, making original use of the public phone box; anyway it was nice to have a bit of a smile while you're working eh? If I was as keen on music hall as I seemed to be, judging off my telephone manner, there was a pub, the Monk's Head, that had it on a Sunday night, perhaps some of the company might enjoy it after we'd settled in? Andy, a slim, quiet young man with a taste for handmade shirts and a thirst like a hod carrier, thought it might be good to 'get the feel of the local audience'; One-amp, who could hold only one idea in her head at a time, was also keen, she'd seen it on TV, and thought the dresses were lovely.

The Stage Manager had assured us it was the real thing, and we found it was, copper-bottomed: an enormous room, with ground-glass globes to the lamps, which had bulbs that flickered as if supplied by uncertain gas-flow, a superb mahogany bar the length of one wall, except for the doors to the lavatories, and also to the dressing-rooms as it turned out, and a small semi-circular stage in the far corner with a faded red curtain, and a piano with the front panel off, at which sat a pugilistic woman with frizzy black dyed hair and a cigarette, punishing the keys with a grim malice; in the shadows round the walls, there were waiters in long white aprons and plastic straw boaters, who would move with discreet skill towards an empty glass before it was back on the table.

As we arrived, a delightful, fresh-complexioned young woman in black fishnet stockings, garters decorated with a small red rose, scarlet tutu, and a well-boned bodice was doing the can-can, solo, frowning in concentration over the routine. Done by a full chorus line, the can-can is only rescued from tawdry humiliation by brazen female arrogance; done solo, by this earnest innocent, it was touching, even brave: like whoring when what you really need is love, a substitute for whatever it was you were aiming at in the first place. The hammering piano made the glasses of beer on the top bounce in rhythm, lending tension to the act it accompanied as the end glass jiggled ever nearer the edge, until the pianist reached up a hand, still vamping with the other, took a drink, and replaced it at the other end.

The curtain didn't close as the dancer ended her spot, but the pianist gave a gladiatorial rah-rah, and the young dancer was mightily applauded, notably by the group from the Lyceum, who recognized the raw truth on the rare occasions that they saw it on stage. The compère shot on, a short ferrety man in a moulting ankle-length rabbit-skin coat and the plastic boater. The landlord must have had a concession. He had a reedy, rapid-fire delivery that sliced through the smoke-laden atmosphere like a buzz-saw: 'Thank you Rita that was our own lovely Rita sorry her lovely partner Maureen couldn't be with us tonight but like I said she's down with the flu on the other side of the Ouse. I can't do the curtain back and forth for our lovely Rita to take another call 'cause as you know, the string broke so I'll just ask you for another round of lovely apple sauce for, Lovely, Rita!'

A darker, more terrible tribal truth was about to be revealed to the audience, but already One-amp was looking lively. She was the sort of Home Counties gel who insisted on getting everything spot-on right. She called the half exactly half an hour before curtain up. Everywhere else it's half an hour before Beginners. Any company she had charge of tended to find themselves hurtling down to the stage half-dressed and wondering where the other three minutes went. It was also almost impossible to stop her correcting the actors on their lines while the show was running. 'Wrong!' she would chirrup, or 'Nothing like it!' She rocked with mirth at the next artiste, under the impression that he was a comic, and she had a point. He had patent leather shoes, with buckles, tartan socks, and a kilt whose colours hurt your eyes. The chrome buckle on his belt was as big as a side-plate, and he had that special gift with lace shirt cuffs, whereby whatever he did with his hands, they were always draped in limp white lace. What to do with your hands on stage can be a problem, but this man had it in spades.

It turned out he was a singer of Scottish ballads, and One-amp had to be calmed down, though the hiccups continued. He had one of those tenor voices that make you wonder if it's you or him, but a few feet from where we sat, and to one side, deep in shadow, he had an enthusiastic audience. He sang 'The Bonnets of Bonnie Dundee' as if an invisible hand was gripping his testicles, and they were delighted. 'Over the Sea to Skye' was a winner. 'I belong to Glasgow' was good enough for La Scala. However, their applause was not as other applause, it was more like the slow, spaced detonations of a twenty-one gun salute, accompanied by savage shouts of approval.

The company's attention, and that of a good deal of the audience was gradually drawn away from Mario MacLanza onstage, to this strange claque. Two of them, one with a large black beard, the other with a large red one. When the singer got to 'My Love is Like a Red Red Rose', the one with the black beard stood up, with a slow and massive dignity. The dim house lights glinted on the silver buttons of his Highland dress jacket, the blanket-pin in the dark green and black kilt, the skean-dhu in his frighteningly hairy socks, and the bright trimmings of his Scottish pipes, in full skirl. It was like the Old Man of Hoy, detaching himself from the mainland.

The tenor stopped giving out with 'My Love is Like a Red Red Rose', as far as anyone could tell. His moist round pink face seemed to have fewer features on it than is usual. His mouth moved around on it freely, like a goldfish in a bowl, mouthing out at a world over which it has no control, mobile, but with nowhere to go. There was a brief pause as the piper mounted the low stage, the

Scottish singer gave him the big hand like a Christian martyr saluting the lion. The red-haired companion, equally magnificently dressed, only in a belligerently khaki jacket, announced fiercely from his seat: 'The Fifth Finest Piper in the World!' One-amp's face shone with a kind of religious awe, 'Daddy was in the Argyll and Sutherlands,' she whispered, hiccups gone. 'I'll tell you what,' said Andy, 'I'll be out front of house every night this week, frisking the punters for migrant bagpipes.'

The piece we were touring was *Ten Little Indians*, single set, french windows. To lend a little landed elegance, Andy had found a sort of sofa for three. The backrest and arms were in the middle, so that wherever you sat, you had your back to the other two. It's called a 'conversational'. Presumably for backbiting. It came in handy for the production. Wilfie, the leading man, was a bit on the short side for the murderous judge.

He was a very good actor indeed. Andy spoke with awe of a time when they'd been rehearsing a drunk scene, with cold water standing in for gin. By the end of the morning Wilfie was genuinely drunk, and had to be shaken out of it by his fellow actors. He had a strong profile, and a waxy pink complexion that you could well imagine dispensing a powerful justice from the Bench, but he'd've had to sit on a big cushion to be seen. In the last scene, when he thinks he's disposed of the hero, which was me, and sets about hanging the heroine, it had been rehearsed that he would step up onto the conversational to gain the extra height he needed to get the fatal noose round her neck. Then the hero rises from the floor, grabs the pistol, and shoots the mad swine dead.

In the flurry of the get-in, nobody much noticed the

ASM knocking six-inch nails into the floor by the Prompt Desk. The resident Stage Manager had rapidly weighed her up, and merely told her to pull the buggers out again at the end of the week. However, dim as she seemed, she proved to know more than the rest of the company, if only about the state of the blanks.

Last scene, I raised the gun as Wilfie throttled away at the heroine, I took aim, carefully slightly upstage of the target, so that the Judge wasn't left with a smoking shirt-front from the wadding of the blank, squeezed the trigger, and a confidence-draining click broke whatever tension the play had managed to engender. A shot will often cause a nervous giggle in an audience, but not a click, and certainly not on a Monday night in Sheffield. Another click, my mind racing neck and neck with Wilfie's for a way out of the emergency: throttle him with his own rope? that seemed to be favourite; while Wilfie, making a rare and gruesome meal of his final foul murder, was thinking 'Heart attack, that'll do it,' and the actress/victim was wondering how far gone in death she'd been acting, and could she convincingly come round and do the old bastard in herself?

And then, from the wings, the leaden clunk of the spare blanks, which One-amp was placing on the six-inch nails, flinching as she hit them one by tedious one with a toffee-hammer, a full box of twenty-five by her side as she knelt to the task. Supposing one of them went off in the middle of my panther-like leap to snatch the rope from the Judge's astonished grasp? what would the audience make of that?

Wilfie, perhaps driven harder by professional desperation than any of us, and spurred on further again by the clang of the Fire Door as Andy hurtled through from front of house, got there first: he clutched his chest with convulsive hands, grinning through a curtain of sweat, a soul tormented, the veins on his forehead standing out like knotted scarlet cord. 'Me heart!' he screamed, jolting the comatose audience into paying attention. He staggered blindly back against the backrest, which carried clear away from its mooring-pegs, and the Judge disappeared upstage with a wild cry of 'Oh for heaven's sake One-amp!'

As the company stood bowing to a subdued audience who were probably as mystified by the mystery play as when they came in, a shot rang out from the wings, and One-amp's clearly enunciated tones could be heard telling a traumatized Andy 'Thought they were a bit damp when I opened them, so I organized back-up.'

The last time I saw Rosie's house, all that remained in a wilderness of demolition were the stone gate pillars, and the front door in its stone surround, all powdered evenly with fine pink brick dust. It seemed to hold a long-lost meaning, a mute guardian of ancient rituals, which in a way, it was. It was easy to see Rosie as the Guardian of the Temple. Small, stooped, with a dark ivory skin like an old withered apple, she looked a hundred and twenty. She said she'd been dresser to Houdini in her youth, and it was easy to believe her. She said the great escapologist was always losing his key and having to wake them up to let him in.

She had a large bathroom, with a vast enamelled cast-iron bath, stained brown by the copper from the boiler. At regular intervals she carried in two large buckets of coal from the yard, giving little yips as she went. The hot water system boomed and boinked late evening, when she'd stoked up the kitchen range, and she would beg her lodgers to take another bath. Only when she had dancers in was the boiler used to anywhere near its fearsome capacity.

I stayed with Rosie again when I was playing King Rat in pantomime, and this time she had three dancers from the show staying, which kept her stoking even more industriously. They had long rowdy baths every weeknight, and thundered up and down stairs, in and out of each other's rooms, giving no sign that they'd just done a stint of work that would have broken the stamina of a plasterer's labourer. Sonny, the comic, was to learn, with their handmaiden help, the hubris that overtakes those whom Dionysius makes mad with pride.

Sonny was playing Dame Whitty, Dick Whittington's mother, and apart from the patter he'd imported from his stand-up act, it wasn't much of a part. He persuaded the management to hire a Kirby's Flying Ballet Harness, so that he would be able to swoop on spectacularly for his first entrance, to the delighted amazement of all. However, to fly convincingly on stage, you have to trust the offstage operator, and Sonny trusted no one. Lucky was a very experienced hand, not much pleased to be hired for one short ego-trip, and having to deal with such a waspish and demanding artiste. The loss of one laugh, or one round of applause, is a death to a stand-up comedian, and Sonny took it out increasingly on Lucky. 'I want to be centre-stage and on my feet at the top of the applause,' he muttered as Lucky harnessed him up in the wings, 'not dangling in mid-air like the last chicken at Sainsbury's; it's my bloody entrance, not yours, and I'm sir.'

Commercial pantomime can look tinselly, the bright pushy costumes, the intrusive microphones, but some of the old magic can still emerge, and this particular night it did. The opening chorus number had the dancers as merry Yorkshire peasants in bright brief dirndls or even briefer lederhosen, singing 'Zippy-di-doo-dah' as they high-kicked away the night's gloom, preparing for the arrival of Dame Whitty; and through the fixed smiles, the military precision of the routine, there shone their gorgeous youth, no disguising the serious devotions they undertook.

'Hello villagers and villageresses,' cried Sonny, and the chorus clapped their hands and cheered happily, falling into their rehearsed positions to give maximum space and power to the Dame. She swooped downstage, all flounces and good humour, carrying a small orange-tasselled parasol high, and wearing a tight candy-striped dress that showed every rib. Rising steeply, she carried straight on out over the orchestra pit, whence the 'Habañera' from *Carmen* now came, *con brio*. 'Ooops,' she cried, 'they'll see me knickers.' An ad-lib, this, and not bad for fast; high on his wire, Sonny had worked it out he was in trouble. 'Put me down you festering plebian,' hissed Widow Whitty as she whirled on by, circled the stage, and out again above the heads of the awestruck stalls, the showbiz grin now fixed in a rictus of rage and despair.

It was all of a piece. The lone fierce piper. The panic-eyed smiling dancers calling out their rehearsed cries of joy and welcome each time Sonny looked like landing. Rosie, creeping about with buckets of coal for the ritual cleansing. The man/woman in mid-air and mid-time, possessed by fury. And Lucky, hauling, grim-faced, on the thick rope that controlled the Flying Harness. 'We'll see who's in charge of what round here.'

'Flying tonight!' screamed the sacrificial goat on the wire, still working on the gag, 'Mushy peas coming up!' Eighth absolute of theatre: don't muck Lucky about.

At the Union Meeting, they conceded, stone-faced, that Lucky was not a part-time stage-hand from the dole-queue. Lucky, for his part said it wouldn't happen again, and most certainly the Dame wasn't a clapped-out club act. I enjoyed the Meeting, as did most of the company, but privately and ruefully I had to conclude that you can rehearse *for* astounding moments, but you can't rehearse them.

Sundays at Rosie's the ritual was different, although still orchestrated by the dancers. Quiet, slow-moving, the bathing even longer. Two of the young women sitting about in purposeless lassitude in the kitchen. Me eating a late breakfast, with the Sunday paper spread out on the table. Rosie leaning against the range, since there wasn't another chair. Poppy, the third dancer, was dragging out a very long soak upstairs, the *News of the World* no doubt sodden in her hands by now, because Maureen and Joyce were trying out each other's nail varnish to fill the aching hours without the titillation of the only Sunday paper they cared to read.

'She did this last week, and the week before,' said Maureen, crouched over her nails.

'I'll dry it out over the oven rail,' said Rosie.

Joyce had finished her nails, and held them out for judgement, 'I don't think it's me do you?' She was corn-gold, the nail varnish was a deep brutal purple, it was certainly striking against her fair freckled skin. The smell of solvent wafted round my breakfast.

'Would you like a bit of the *Observer*?' I said.

'It's all articles isn't it?' said Maureen, 'no pictures, nothing you can read.'

I tried again, '*Citizen Kane*'s on at the Odeon.'

'Seen it,' said Joyce, 'what you think Maureen? it's not me is it? Nah.' She took one of the tissues on the table between them and wiped the varnish off with speed, then contemplated her nails again, 'Ah now Maureen, now see what you've gone and let me do; I went and wiped it off didn't I? I could have let it dry and then picked it off, it'd been something to do.'

Rosie's spade-shaped wireless, with its bronze switch like a light-switch and which was never off except when she got someone in to change a valve, tinkled faintly on its high shelf by the chimney-breast, draped in cobwebs that were probably pre-war too. I was very fond of the temporary sisterhood I'd joined, they were good people, innocent, hard-working, underpaid; but I also wanted urgently to work my way through the dazzling perceptions of Ken Tynan's theatre review, telling me of that other, high-flying drama, that was as far above my own aspirations as Sonny in full flight. I could better understand the grim epic realities of Brecht in Berlin, which I had found in translation, than the mellifluent, unbloodied elegance of the Shakespeare Memorial Theatre I'd seen at Stratford. Once again, I found myself finding my new horizons in the written word.

Then Poppy's footsteps passed heavily overhead and thumped down the stairs to the kitchen, pink, her hair damp and dishevelled about her face, and tossed the limp smudgy newspaper onto the table.

'I'll get another chair from the front room,' said Rosie.

'Don't bother,' said Poppy, 'I'll stand.'

'Not to your breakfast surely?'

'I'll *stand*,' said the dancer, through compressed lips, and moved painfully to the side of the range.

'You all right Poppy?' said Joyce, waving her fingers to dry another experimental nail varnish, 'you sound funny.'

'I was shaving my legs in the bath, as you do . . .'

'Go on then? You're *hobbling*, Polly.'

'Nicked me clit, didn't I?' she said.

9

Theatres should have markets next: drama with stars and no text

The boys in the yard jostled round me, shoving, jeering, flicking at my tie. I was back in the nightmare playground at Southport, the pale, buck-toothed, spindly little evacuee, a Manchester sparrow dropped into the wrong nest. Thirty years old by now, but I recognized the same empty abandonment in a grey, blurred, incomprehensible world. This time as Prisoner D, the Boy from the Isles, in Behan's *The Quare Fellow*, Theatre Royal, in the East End of London.

There might have been a script. There were vague references to a ragbag collection of anecdotes and newspaper articles that had been cobbled together for a Dublin production. I even glimpsed a couple of pages of typed dialogue, but the improvisations threw me. I'd become reasonably skilled in performance, presentation, punching home a scene so that everybody knows what's going on. A number of the company had worked together for years, and were awesomely skilled, but in ways new to me. Dance, mime, music, nothing seemed beyond them. I'd seen them in *Edward II*, a play I knew quite well, and Marlowe's lines came over vividly. What for me had been a one-D, single-theme story now unfolded with a powerful human and political dimension I'd never noticed. If the Executioner has any lines, they're certainly not many, but his arachnid presence, watching the tormented King, was terrifying. But there was no doubt there was a script. *The Quare Fellow* seemed uncharted.

No, I had to conclude, in the few moments I ever got to myself, like on the Tube, this way of working was not performance, this was the real thing. Maybe a performance might be carved out of it later, I didn't know, and was too damn busy to ask, but right now all I had to hang onto was the uncertainty, that I was as uncertain as Prisoner D. I knew in my ham bones that performance was truth: it is true that I am standing here, on this stage, in a prison uniform from Wardrobe, talking to you as part of a story, now.

From Coco's Crazy Car routine on, I'd known that this is a completely involving experience. I took pride in the skills I'd learnt, and thought them every bit as valuable as an engineer's, if not quite so well paid. What I wasn't ready for was the disappearance of Henry, and the lumpish, hovering, unsure presence of the Boy from the Isles, whose name I didn't even know. Outside, the hoarse, cheerful shouts of the traders of the Angel Lane Market; inside the theatre, the cold, grim and dull boredom of Mountjoy Jail.

It probably started in the Manager's office. Gerry was a large, genial man, with glossy dark curly hair and a flamboyant moustache, which he tended to finger in the manner of a villain in melodrama. He successfully concealed his beginnings as the son of a Manchester businessman, and as the golden boy of his generation at

Manchester Grammar School. He was also an impressive actor, with a powerful presence, and rumbustious good company. However, the long hard trek that had brought Theatre Workshop to some international recognition had taught him an impressive lexicon of financial ploys and evasions. 'We don't have a fixed wage, we share equally at the Box Office receipts,' he told me.

'So how much is that just now?'

'About eight pounds.'

I calculated that I could just about live off that, and accepted.

Come the first Friday, Gerry counted four pounds into my hand. It took me a few seconds to believe what had just happened.

'What do I do for the other four pounds?'

'You go to the Labour Exchange. Is there anybody else waiting outside?' So that's why rehearsals were a bit thin on Wednesdays and Fridays: Dole days. Even the wages were improvised.

As I continued to work in the East End, I found that haunted figures would accost me from time to time on Mile End tube station. I remembered them individually as they stood before me, but could recall little of them afterwards. 'You're working at Theatre Workshop?'

'Yes.'

'And you're a writer, as well as being an actor?'

'Yes.'

'I'm a writer myself. They stole my research/father's songs/my radio idea. Not an acknowledgement, not a penny you know.'

I'd heard a fine and moving radio programme based on World War I soldiers' songs, interspersed with the news of casualties and ground gained. One of the casualties was to be met on Mile End tube station. But nothing could compare with the Theatre Workshop *Oh What a Lovely War*; the film version, with proper attribution, is a shadow by comparison. It was difficult for me to find an adequate response to these earnest, wounded men who had seen their efforts and talents turned into near masterpieces, without so much as a nod in their direction.

I knew the straits Theatre Workshop had navigated in their early days, touring the Welsh and Pennine valleys in beat-up old vans and lorries. They'd devised their first shows between them, anything copyright was ignored, not accounted for; how can you account for ten per cent of nothing? They'd lived on porridge on occasions. Even the floodlights had been looted from a crashed USAF reconnaissance plane on the Derbyshire moors. And there were these figures on the tube station between trains, looking for justice in a harsh world. The doors slid open and then closed again, I went dumbly on my way.

Joan, the Director, asked Brendan to tell the company about the murder which led up to the sentence of death which is carried out in the play. He began, 'The various nations commit murder for various reasons. The French might do it for *la gloire*, or the old *amour*. Or the Englishman for instance, would kill you for Queen and Country, or for the advancement of trade. But your true Gael,' he said, 'will only commit murder for noble and patriotic reasons, like a couple a hundred acres of potatoes.'

His bardic description of the brothers and their dispute on the farm, culminating in the one slaughtering the other in a slather of blood; the young lad visiting from the next farm as the corpse was being butchered for disposal, ending with 'Did you kill a pig Barney?' 'I did so,' says your man. 'Would you ever let me have a bit off the leg?' spiralled off into a myth whose brutal details were so graphically narrated that they had to be true. The Quare Fellow, that's to say the condemned man, doesn't appear in the play, but for the prisoners in Mountjoy Jail, he was a blood-boltered presence.

It was a bit like being in a pack of hounds in hot pursuit. No one seemed to have a clear idea of what it was we were pursuing, though Joan, the Director, sometimes may have done. We worked for two tedious days on the grave-digging scene, where the Boy from the Isles hotly and uncertainly defends the Quare Fellow against the crude abuse of the other cons, because he's met him on remand, and likes him. It wasn't working, and I fell back on the old twice-nightly trick of upstaging for my outburst, more out of weariness than in hopes of satisfying Madam. Deep down, she might have known that such a crude trick would do it, but to suggest anything so artificial, when the search was on for the truth, would have been an impossible mental contortion, even to a mind as devious as hers.

The company began to sense that the scent was chest-high, but what was the quarry? Theatre Workshop had had some Continental success, in Czechoslovakia, Sweden, and a towering reception at the Paris Festival with *Arden of Faversham* the previous year. And *The Good Soldier Schweik* had had a respectable run in the West End. Was this the chance for them to break out of the encircling disdain of many British critics, the clubby disparagement of the Arts Council? Joan . . 'Jay Hell', as she signed herself on runic postcards to friends, would take a revival of *Schweik* to the Paris Festival.

I was barely aware of all this. Grand designs were not among my emotional furniture. I knew a full house was better than half a dozen and a comp on a wet Wednesday matinee in Arbroath, but the idea of setting out to storm an international festival was not within my experience. Ambition had evaporated from my empty lungs when I hurled myself off the lighting bridge. Now all I wanted was to get it right.

There was a short break before a week's running-in of *Schweik* at Oxford, so I took the chance to visit my mother. The gun was making me uneasy in London. Gangsterism was keeping level with the housing market, and a shotgun, even one as crummy as my father's, was getting to be a fashion accessory for a rack-renter's minder, sawn-off. It would be safer among the fluff. I slid out of my mother's house on the Friday before I was due in Oxford, the gun under my coat, the family collie at my heels, to take advantage of the morning pigeon flight. The sky was duck-egg blue between the high beeches, with scudding cloud way up. For an hour or more there was not a movement. Then, at eleven o'clock, the woodpigeon started to pass over me in small groups of two or three, to drop into a cornfield next to me. I waited, still. As soon as there were around ten in the corn, with one look-out bird at the top of the field's hedge, I knew I could take the next pair coming in, reload, take the look-out and the first bird up from the corn, reload, and maybe another two as they swirled up.

The gun had a dotted line of yellowing white enamel along the rib. When I closed and lifted the gun, and the dotted line joined up with the flight-line of the bird, the bird was dead in the air. The dog was as tense as a coiled spring as the latecomers began to arrive over our heads. It hated the detonations of the ancient dried-out cartridges, but loved its own skill in seeking out the dead birds and retrieving them. I glanced down briefly. Two young rabbits, ten feet from me, raising their heads, moist noses folding and unfolding, questing to know where this new treat had come from since they last passed that way. I must have been totally immobile for an hour.

Then they came, grey specks, high, but unmistakably the powerful arrow-straight flight of woodpigeon. I turned my back to the approaching birds, waiting for them to spot the others feeding on the ground. They passed over the copse, seemed almost to stop in the air for a second before dipping to glide in; crash-crash, two pigeon folded and dropped into the ride at the edge of the copse; reload, the barrels now hot to touch, the dog cringing away from the next barrage to come; crash-crash, two more from the flock as it rose in confusion, the dog now in a strung fever, shaking, frantic to pick up; reload, my fingers fumbling with haste for the last chance, crash – and then, the loudest explosion I've ever heard, including the Bofors gun at the end of the road during the Manchester Blitz; so loud it resembled silence.

The barrels blew apart, the wood of the fore-end lay about my feet, made matchsticks, the butt, trigger and guard were all that remained in my tingling hands, no hammers, no sign of the four pound of steel that had been the barrels. The collie had gone, and was as suddenly before me again, a woodpigeon in its mouth. It dropped the bird at my feet, since I made no effort to take it, and had collected the other four before my benumbed senses had begun to work out what had happened. My grandfather would have known; if my father knew, he was too taciturn a man to mention it; the old gun wasn't proofed for modern nitro cartridges: it was a time-bomb, waiting to go off.

During that apocalyptic millisecond when I didn't know whether I was alive or a nothing, together with the wrap-round vigilance of the last couple of hours, the detail of leaves lifting in the breeze to show their undersides, telling me which way the birds would turn to land and take off, the scan of the wide sky, looking for specks that would become a flock, I also saw, or rather experienced, the previous three months of first the rehearsal period and then the unfolding performances of *The Quare Fellow*. Unlike most of the company, for me it had been a crash course in epic theatre. No other company in England, and few elsewhere, were doing anything like it: drama that was ritual, total, and yet at the same time acute reportage of documented experience. Maybe I did have a glimmer of ambition after all, if I was still alive. I would prepare for, and resonate to, I told myself grandly, the stillness that's at the centre of clowning.

Even among the toffee papers underneath the seating at the circus, writhing and jerking in an ecstasy of laughter, I knew that Coco's hands were relaxed and easy, the stance and movements precise, graceful in the baggy trousers and slapshoes, balletic without the intense muscularity and effort of classical dance. Considering what a clumsy self-conscious clodhopper I was, even I could see that my ambition was overweening, but wasn't it after all what most human beings wanted? To be glad to wake in a morning, to look forward to the day's work? To feel fulfilled at the end of it? Otherwise you really are dead. Jay Hell detected and rejected acting-for-effect with the same dismissive contempt that a stonemason has for 'jumpers' in face-work (stones set on edge with the grain vertical, to save having to plumb every course) . . . a wall has strength in its structure, not in its surface appearance.

Brian was another outsider in the company for *The Quare Fellow*. He was also one of the few Irishmen in the cast, and suffered fiercely from Catholic guilt; he paid a prostitute thirty shillings a week to relieve him of it; 'No physical contact, d'you see?' he explained, his eyes wide and hot. He had a bold out-front delivery, like a comic's feed, slamming his lines at the audience with the rough vigour of a hurley player. Joan was happy to accommodate his energy, and knew anyway that the enclosed world of prison throws up some rum buggers, exaggerates eccentricity within its rigid structure, but one of the scenes, in which he was the Prison Visitor pestered by the old lag Dunlavin for a room to go to and a handout on his release, wasn't happening, there seemed to be no core to it, no through-line, an end-of-pier double act would have been more convincing. Suddenly she shouted 'Play it the man's desperate for a pee.' And the scene took off: the actor had a purpose, to get the hell off that landing, you could almost see the long flight of stone steps to the nearest lavatory. It was twenty years before I fully realized what a stroke of genius went into that brief scene: when you first see Dunlavin, he's polishing his cell chamber-pot.

Mountjoy Jail. The long wait for dawn, and a barbarous death in the morning. The actors playing prisoners are up on the fly gallery, staring down intently into a pool of white light from the single lamp in the exercise yard. Such concentration of hundreds of eyes creates a powerful silence. Two warders wait for the Hangman and his assistant, who finally arrive late, and drunk. The Hangman lost his little black box in one of the pubs between the docks and the jail, and they've had to revisit all of them again to find it. The Hangman has had a look into the Condemned Cell, and concludes that the Condemned Man has an unusually thick neck, and reworks his calculations, back to the audience, a silhouette, bulky, dark, bowler-hatted, adding another couple of inches to the drop. Meanwhile, his assistant accompanies himself on the melodeon . . .

> My brother, si-i-i-it and thi-ink.
> While yet some time is left to thee
> Kneel to thy God who from thee does not shrink
> And lay thy sins on Him who died for thee.

HANGMAN: Take a fourteen-stone man as a basis and giving him a drop of eight foot . . .

The good-nights are exchanged.

The yard falls to night-time silence. Prisoner C sings 'She walked through the fair' in Gaelic, high up in the Cell Block, a keening beautiful wake for a man few of them have known.

Stillness, dark, every eye stretched wide.

And then

A jump-cut as thunderous as a trip hammer, lights full up at one slam, and the Irish National Anthem blares out, full volume. It was as if the whole building, all of

Dublin City, was being wound up to a pitch of intolerable tension. Two warders on day duty, stiff, vigilant, the only move when one checks his watch: half a minute to go. Screw. Screw.

And then

A prisoner's voice, way up, giving a race-track commentary on the progress of the Hanging Party. 'We're ready for the start, and in good time and who do I see lined up for the off but the High Sheriff of this ancient city of ours . . . and we're off, in this order: the Governor, two screws Regan and Crimmin the quare fellow between them two more screws and three runners from across the Channel, getting well in front now the Canon. The quare fellow's got the white pudding bag on his head, just a short distance to go and he's making a big effort for the last two furlongs and he's in! His feet to the chalk line now he'll be pinioned, the bag pulled down over his face two screws come off the trap and steady him Himself goes to the lever and . . .' From every part of the jail a ferocious feral howling, 'One off, one away, one off, one away, one off one away, one off one away . .'

How could an explosion that so obliterated my senses so sensitize my mind that it seemed to encompass more than at any other time in my life? As I plucked and dressed the six pigeon, I didn't know which explosion either, the gun, or the Hanging. It must be the sort of experience mystics try to tell, so improbable they're very likely true. After the first night, the Front of House Manager told Behan he'd better change that National Anthem segue, there'd been a goodly sprinkling of Irish in the audience who thought the English were being unusually respectful towards them and that this was the end of the show, so they stood up.

'Me mother wrote it,' said Behan, 'if I can't use it, nobody can. There's this writer called MacDonagh, he's a magistrate down in County Cork. He claims he wrote it, but he didn't, it was the mother. I've thought about going down there to his court, and when he's saying "I fine you in the sum of ten shillings for stealing a pig . ." I'll shout out, "What about you stealing me mother's song?" '

For a moment, as I stowed the pigeon and the remains of the gun into carrier bags, I thought I'd stumbled on the ninth absolute of theatre; I couldn't quite formulate it, but it must be somewhere in among that astonishing piece of hokum Jay Hell had sprung; something about 'No such thing as a one-man show'? But it didn't work: Behan was a one-man show in himself. He probably told himself stories in his sleep.

The Quare Fellow was a success with critics, and audiences were coming; it was to open at the Comedy Theatre in the West End immediately after the Paris Festival; in Paris, *Schweik* was to play the Sarah Bernhardt, one of the biggest and grandest theatres in Paris. Theatre Workshop tilted and rose on the crest of a very big wave, I could feel the thrust of it, and knew the damage of that tilt: with much of the male talent they could draw on tied up in the West End, what happened to the ensemble work in Stratford on which the company was based? West End money, international prestige, were sorely needed to underpin the work, but who would there be to continue the work in the East End? More than that, Stratford E15 would become a lift-off platform for actors who were fiercely ambitious in altogether different ways to Theatre Workshop's.

Mind, the grubby stratagems that from time to time took my breath away continued, prosperity or no. The scenery for *Schweik* was packed late Saturday night and Sunday morning by the company after the Oxford week. It was to go, all two tons of it, twelve-foot tongue and groove panels, a revolve, two baskets of costumes and one of rifles, Passenger's Luggage in Advance.

Gerry even bought an extra ticket for Gerard's wife, Shirley, an apparently generous act which actually made up the numbers so as to take advantage of British Railways' unwitting free service. I was given £15 expenses to go ahead and organize its safe arrival. I sat in the Oxford Playhouse Green Room, full of foreboding; I'd had previous experience of French bureaucracy, and suspected they might not be quite so amenable as their British colleagues. Gerry had arranged for the customs officer to inspect and seal the crated scenery and costumes at the Playhouse. This way, the Revenue wouldn't know they were party to a fraud, and the Railway Goods Department wouldn't know what it was they were carrying.

'Watch the door,' said Gerry, so I did. There was a rattle and a clatter, and I glimpsed a shower of change crash and spill into Gerry's hands from the payphone box, before glancing back in alarm to the door, where stood, as if drawn by invisible strings, a large Oxford policeman, his eyes round with moral indignation.

'Is that your car outside sir?'

'Yes,' muttered Gerry, his broad bulk sturdily in front of the phone, money carpeting the ground round his feet.

'You can't do that sir! You can't move a No Parking sign the length of your car, and just . . *park.*'

Gerry moved towards the door at speed, stuffing enough keys to break into San Quentin back in his pocket, 'I'll shift it, there's some valuable papers in it, didn't want to leave it too long. Thank you officer.'

Three days to get two tons of *matériel théâtral*, disguised as personal effects, across the Channel and into the Sarah Bernhardt Theatre in the middle of Paris. Every step along the way, from the Communist dockyard foreman at Boulogne to the Import/Export Licence Officer at Batignolles Railway Depot in Paris, blithe hope and dull despair beat systole and diastole in my heart. What a bottle Gerry had mixed for me, multi-coloured forms in quintuplicate, taxi-rides to addresses I couldn't make out, scribbled for me on scraps of paper (one very well-turned-out agent offered to take the whole grim business off my hands for £800, and came down to £80 in the three days), hour after hour sitting waiting on wooden benches in dim-lit corridors outside tall narrow offices, with windows way up, giving the rooms a green light that dampened my spirits, a £100 bond to find, where the hell was I going to find a hundred thousand francs? In the end, I borrowed it as a blank cheque off a friendly UNESCO man, feeling like a conman as I did so . . he wouldn't lose his money, that is unless Gerry somehow made a deal to sell the *matériel* in Paris, but all the same . .

After three days, I became quite friendly with the customs officer at Batignolles, the goods depot for Paris; he even helped me fill in the forms which he then inspected to see if they were properly filled in. And then, with two hours to go before the company arrived at the Gare du Nord on the other side of town, the *douanier* suddenly threw up his hands and said 'You can't sign, you're not a French national!' £800 that agent had asked, for signing a piece of paper. The *douanier* signed five times, shook me by the hand, and wished the company success in the Festival.

Grey with sleeplessness and anxiety, I met the boat train, having made sure all the hotel bookings were firm, the wagon of *matériel* was standing at the *Bagages* platform at Gare du Nord. I ushered the company into a battered old coach, which had a chalked sign saying 'Theatre Worrettkshotte' because I couldn't remember on the phone how you say 'k' in French; every time I said 'Uh . .', the woman wrote down 'e', 'Er, erm, kay, k-kay, non! ka,' I stuttered, and we chugged off into the rush-hour traffic, the driver yelling over the thunderous clatter of the engine 'What type of lunatic orders a coach to cross Paris at five in the afternoon?' That night, I slept as dreamless a sleep as I had after the party in the ugly little house by Belfast Lough. Sometimes, the stillness that's at the centre of clowning can seem more like emptiness.

Backstage staff with Theatre Workshop was minimal. Camel on lighting, and whoever was available for any other job, so that everyone knew the show, and there were few errors. There was a small incident in *Macbeth*, when Joan had a notion to set a floodlight moon to illuminate Lady Macbeth's face as she made her exit from the sleepwalking scene. The actress wasn't expecting it, and blindly descended the ten-foot drop without the aid of the ladder, followed by a resounding thud, and a gasp of pain and astonishment. 'Will she now go to bed?' the doctor asks the gentlewoman attending her. 'Directly,' she replies.

Generally speaking, staging was simple. For *Schweik*, the final artillery barrage was represented by a brilliant flash of white light in darkness, with a clash of cymbals for the detonations. I translated for Camel: 'When madame clashes the cymbals,' I translated, as Camel mumbled that sheepish kind of English that often comes out in the presence of foreigners, 'could we have a flash of the most white light you've got? It's to represent cannonfire.' 'Certainly,' the electrician called down from his bridge, 'when does she clash the cymbals?' I asked Camel, and translated the reply: 'She clashes the cymbals when she clashes the cymbals.' The electrician had already locked his board and was on his way down as I was speaking. He looked me straight in the eye, the look of a man who's just heard a certain suggestion about his wife. 'Midi,' he said, and disappeared for two hours. When he came back, he was a lot calmer.

The opening Gala Night was packed with elegance, and a sturdy contingent from UNESCO. The revolve revolved in its tongue and groove frame, each time showing a new cartoon to back the new scene, the costumes' black and white adding to the overall effect of cartoon, like a black and white Pollock's Toy Theatre; it ought not to have worked, it was much more brutally anti-authority than Hašek's genial stories. Joan conducted a violent argument throughout the show with a French fascist two rows in front of her. But there were bursts of applause, laughter, and, barring the running row in the stalls, keen attention. The immense red velvet curtain swooshed down at the end. The company lined up to take their bow, civilized applause, curtain down again, and immediately up again, and again, and again.

The actors begin to see the backs of departing dinner suits and gowns, the thud of rising tip-up seats begins to compete with the loyal applause, and still the curtain rises and falls relentlessly, like the Flyman's Revenge. I remembered with a chill the time the curtain fell at Leicester at the end of a rumbustious knockabout farce, and rose again on complete silence. The night at Sheffield when a man fell fast asleep into the aisle during Noël Coward. A Navaho steel erector, or an oil platform roustabout may have a statistically higher chance of dying at work, but dying onstage is a high risk, not fatal, but it's dire, and the grief is deadening, personal and permanent.

The next day, the theatre critic of *Le Figaro* roundly declared that *The Good Soldier Schweik* was a triumph. There hadn't been a publication of *Schweik* in France for many years. The author's own cartoons show Schweik to be a thickset dog thief with a head like a potato. Max, Theatre Workshop's hero, had been described as looking like a Belgian whippet, all prick and claws. His depiction of the central devious scrimshanker, was, according to *Le Figaro*, Hašek to the life. The company were puzzled, but accepted fortune's favour graciously, took tea with the British Ambassador, and strolled along the Faubourgs as if they'd just bought them, though in fact they could barely afford a croissant.

'I suppose you fellows can take it easy now eh?' remarked the diplomat with Jermyn Street shoes creased like an old paper bag, 'savour your success, and drink your meed of praise?' My mind strayed from the rose-petal strewn garden to backstage at the Sarah Bernhardt, Joan bollocking the company comprehensively and individually for meretricious mugging, slack attention and staying up all night on the duty-free.

'Well,' I said, 'it's not all that easy, we're re-rehearsing a show for the Comedy.'

'Lovely little bijou theatre,' said the man, 'I always feel terribly at home there d'you know?'

Brendan did his best to keep his play in the public mind while the company was in Paris and then at Brighton to run in *The Quare Fellow*. On a BBC TV chat show, he so jostled the urbane sang-froid of the host that a phone call was put through from Hospitality to the Director-General at home to say they had a drunken Irish author on their hands, should they drop him from the programme? No, said the DG gravely, don't drop him, but if he says 'Fuck', don't laugh. Brendan made the front page of the *Daily Mirror*, tousled curls, white shirt open to his navel.

He did his Dublin jackeen impersonation of a Synge play, with his soft tweed jacket pulled up over his head as a shawl. 'Oh me father's cone,' he keened, 'me brothers is all cone, me uncles and me cousins, and me aunt Nellie's nephew's sons, cone, cone . . . (You'd think the old biddie was selling ice-cream with all these cones about the place . .) Ach the carpenter will be bringing the clane boards . . (I ask you this, what kind of a man would he be to go out looking for *dirty* boards to make a coffin?)' This by way of illustrating his distaste for stage Irishry. And there he was, full page, national press, his delicate Irish lips curling round the F-word. Received thought is that Kenneth Tynan was the first on television, but he wasn't. He was the first that anyone could make out.

One of the recruits for the West End was a rising young Irish actor, just out of drama school. Nobody else knew he was rising, but he did. His was a smallish part, Mixer, a dangerous and hardened con. There's a longish speech from Neighbour, a crumbling, meths-soaked old lag, in which he slavers over the grand breakfast the Condemned Man will be having in the dawn of the next day. The stage is still, except for the trembling senile relish of Neighbour. Mixer chose this moment to cross, with restless, barely controlled foul temper, and spit, downstage centre of Neighbour.

Joan presumably accepted this as spontaneous. She was certainly penetratingly shrewd. If she detected the crude attention-seeking ambition, she was possibly watching the acting-for-effect for its effect. She called an afternoon note session in Brighton. Mixer sent word that he was in London for a film test. She still didn't comment. It was a low-key discussion, for her. The grave-digging scene was taken apart, ostensibly to reaffirm the through-line, more likely it was to rattle complacency.

That evening, the scene was a shambles, each actor desperately feeding the lines in at random, as if all they wanted was to get to firm ground. Certainly any complacency I had had was thoroughly rattled. The hot confused outburst of Prisoner D was heartfelt. Until we got to Neighbour's catalogue of the Quare Fellow's breakfast. I watched Mixer detach himself from the far wall of the Exercise Yard, and set off to make a little world for himself onstage as usual.

Suddenly I detected the through-line: the Condemned Man's breakfast. Yes. The cons in the Yard were pawns in a game being played elsewhere; it all fell into place. I became mesmerized by the grisly speech, drawn closer to Neighbour, and then stopped to listen even more intently, right on the spot selected by Mixer for his spit for stardom. Out of the corner of my eye, I saw the rising young actor halt, a look of freezing unfeigned homicidal hatred on his face. I was just thinking that if the hard man so much as moved a knuckle I'd deck him where he stood, then Mixer gave up the stand-off. For ever. Joan's snort of glee could be heard clear from the back of the stalls.

Twenty pounds a week. Four clean, white fivers. Afternoons in the Oasis open-air swimming pool, surrounded by brown and beautiful showgirls and chorus boys in itsy-bitsy bikinis. In those sunlit days, I wasn't at all sure about it. I could eat now in the restaurants where I once toiled into the night. I could order a bottle of house wine, and *petto di pollo*, chat with the Manageress over coffee and Zabucco. I worked at the writing, even began to sell the odd script. So why did I feel reality was somewhere out there, beyond my grasp?

Gerard, playing Neighbour, had done his research for the part around the Paddington Canal Basin, and other dumps for life's leftovers. That had been real all right, in fact he came back catatonic from one excursion. He'd settled down next to one stinking heap of rags and carrier-bags. The man asked if he came from the North? No, he was Welsh. 'I had a mucker once who was Welsh,' said the man through his bristles and pustules, 'I loved that man, loved him. Here, have a drink.'

Gerard took the meths with dread in his heart. The

man seemed to have relapsed into memories of friendship past. Gerard put his thumb over the neck of the bottle, tipped it to his mouth swiftly, shuddered as convincingly as he knew how, and handed it back. 'Ta, good stuff that,' he said, gasping and blinking as much from the thought of the liquor as the cat's piss whiff the man gave off. The derelict's face dissolved in grief. He wailed to the other figures humped by smouldering fires, 'He dinnernt 'rink i'. I offere' 'im a 'rink 'n 'e dinnernt 'rink i',' blubbing painfully.

Gerard left in a cold sweat. Now, onstage, the ghost of the Paddington Basin haunted his performance, his stubbly grimy chin coated with slimy dribbles from the effects of poisonous liquor. The comfortable West End audience watched respectfully as the scenes of degradation, lowlife and human resilience unfolded. Then one lady was moved to involuntary response. 'What's that he's got on his chin?' and immediately answered her own question, 'Eu-ugh'.

I sat at my little table in Euston, eating toast, the tea shimmering in my mug as the trains rumbled by below, the radio burbling. 'And now over to our Oldham correspondent, who is talking to a local stage hypnotist and publican,' it said. Galvanized, I reached to turn up the volume against the clatter of distant wheels.

'Now, Richard, I understand you propose to hypnotize the entire Rochdale Hornets rugby team for their Derby match against Oldham tomorrow?'

'Yes That Is True. Jim.'

'Won't that take rather a long time, thirteen players?'

'Fifteen Players. Jim. There's Two Reserves to Be Motivated for Success Al-so.'

'Fifteen players? So how long to hypnotize each man?'

'A Matter of Seconds Per Man. Jim. You Gaze In-to My Eyes, and I Say You Are Going to Sleep, You Are Going To Sleep . . .'

Then, the phoniest snores I had ever heard on stage or in life emerged from the little trannie to my astonished ears.

'You Are Now Think-ing You Are a Dog,' intoned Richard.

'Wuff-wuff,' said the interviewer, 'wuff-wuff.'

'When I Snap my Fingers, You Will Wake Up and Sing "Rule Britannia".'

'Rule Britannia, Britannia rules the waves,' sang the interviewer before the studio cross-faded him with *Thought for the Day*.

I went down to collect my mail in a daze. A letter. From the Royal Shakespeare Company. A contract. They would do my play. 'Boom.' Directed by the Artistic Director. 'Boom boom.' Designed by Camel. 'Boom boom boom.' Nobody came out of their rooms to investigate; the dingy hallway echoed with silence. So I boomed again. It was as if I was following Carroll's White Rabbit to strange encounters that would eventually show some kind of subterranean meaning. Richard's amber eyes burned in my mind, as if searching for the person in there, but any understanding I reached lasted no longer than what seemed to be seconds of somebody else's time. If the core of self is what other people make of you, then I couldn't imagine that anybody thought about me long enough to register a whole person. Why should they? What did I know of Coco's home life? I was a performance, no more, no less. The bizarre broadcast from Oldham echoed in my mind, and I remembered shouting into my grandma's empty rain barrel, a solitary boy in an experience I thought no one else in the whole world had ever had or would ever have. 'Boom-boom.'

Outside the Stratford-on-Avon sceneshop, I chanced on Paddy, the Company's Technical Manager. Paddy was watching anxiously as a set was being loaded into two pantechnicons for the London base. It was my set. A huge marine boiler, made, for stage purposes out of sections of ten-ply wood, cladded with hessian and painted to represent steel and steam-insulation. It was wondrously 'practical', and would judder into action, feeding itself coal, and registering steam-pressure on a huge gauge.

It eventually dominated the Aldwych stage, a brooding presence which attacked various people, including the Director; during a technical run, the glass of the gauge shattered and a shard glanced off his shoulder and came near to filleting his arm. If I ever visited backstage during the run, the crew that worked it booed me; they had to inhabit it during the show, working the coal feeders, the gauge, the steam and coal, besides having to dismantle the damn thing to make way for other plays in the repertoire, and then put it up again. I hoped the booing was jocular, the overtime must have been colossal.

I discovered later that Paddy had been a Commando officer during the war, much revered for his calm good humour under battle stress. No one had ever heard him say a harsh word. He was wincing now as the sections of boiler were eased over the tailboard: would they even *fit*?

'That's mine,' I said, 'my dream, fulfilled by a dream technical staff, a dream designer, and a dream director with a dream cast.' Perhaps success wasn't so hollow after all. The setting sun burnished Paddy's greying hair back to the gold it must once have been, his fine-boned Roman profile seemed luminous. He may have glanced at me, but his attention was on the boiler.

'It was a marine boiler when it set off, before it was a dyeworks boiler I mean. Camel went to a dyeworks, and made a machine drawing, and squared it up in the Workshop. For my play.'

'Fuck off,' said Paddy.

As it happened, it didn't attack anyone on the first night. It blew up at the end, spewing steam and coal over the cast, but that was what it was supposed to do. There had been a notion, briefly canvassed, that most of the cast would be fed down the coal hoppers when the machine goes berserk at the end. It was the kind of ruthless sight-gag I relished, but nobody else did, so it was elbowed.

It was a very grand first night, champagne in the elegant bars, evening dress, white tie, and a sprinkling, I was to discover later, of Covent Garden traders and porters on comps. The play's theme, insofar as it had one, was a world without work. It was prophetic. Work-shy young man applies for a vacancy in the dyeworks which is fully automated. All he has to do is press a button twice a shift. 'When do I get a break?' he asks the

Manager. 'A break? You get no break. How the devil can you take a break from doing nothing?'

After the show, the buzz was good. I treated myself to a pint of draught Guinness in the nearest pub, and earwigged on earnest, and, I hoped, approving chat as silks and studded starched shirt-fronts rustled up the stairs to the restaurant above. A big shiny man in a suit that was so superbly cut that he must have had a fitting for every stitch in it, held my eye. He came over and squared up to me, and demanded to know was it right I wrote the show? I admitted it, warily. Him and the boys, he indicated his friends with a vast hand, worked on the market. They sometimes got comps, fill up the house see? Make a first night look better. They'd enjoyed tonight, but what was all these penguins chattering on about significance? Him and the boys thought it was just a good laugh.

I was defensive. 'Perhaps it's their idea of a fun night out, they like the chatter,' I said. 'It's not a criminal activity.'

'Load a cobblers,' said my new friend. 'A good larf, that's what it was, wannit?'

As Behan said, 'You could sing that, if you had an air to it.'